THE LANGUAGE OF PHILOSOPHY

MARTINUS NIJHOFF PHILOSOPHY LIBRARY

VOLUME 4

1. D. Lamb, Hegel – From Foundation to System
   ISBN 90 247 2359 0

2. I.N. Bulhof, William Dilthey – A hermeneutic approach to the study of history and culture
   ISBN 90 247 2360 4

3. W.J. van der Dussen, History as a Science: The Philosophy of R.G. Collingwood
   ISBN 90 247 2453 8

4. M. Chatterjee, The Language of Philosophy
   ISBN 90 247 2372 8

5. E.-H. Kluge, The Metaphysics of Gottlob Frege
   ISBN 90 247 2422 8

6. D. Dutton and M. Krausz, eds., The Concept of Creativity
   ISBN 90 247 2418 X

ISBN series 90 247 2344 2

THE LANGUAGE OF PHILOSOPHY

by

MARGARET CHATTERJEE

1981

MARTINUS NIJHOFF PUBLISHERS

THE HAGUE/BOSTON/LONDON

Distributors:

for the United States and Canada
Kluwer Boston Inc.
190 Old Derby Street
Hingham, MA 02043
U.S.A.

for further information
Martinus Nijhoff Publishers b.v.
P.O.B. 566
2501 CN The Hague
The Netherlands

for India, Sri Lanka and Nepal
Allied Publishers Private Ltd.
Postbox 155
New Delhi – 110002
India

for all other countries
Kluwer Academic Publishers Group
Distribution Centre
P.O.B. 322
3300 AH Dordrecht
The Netherlands

First published in 1981 by Allied Publishers Pvt. Ltd., India

ISBN 90 247 2372 8 (this volume)
ISBN 90 247 2344 2 (Series)

Copyright © 1981 by Margaret Chatterjee

All rights reserved. No part of this publication may be reproduced, stored in a retrieval system, or transmitted in any form or by any means, mechanical, photocopying, recording, or otherwise, without the prior written permission of the publisher, Martinus Nijhoff Publishers, P.O. Box 566, 2501 CN The Hague, The Netherlands.

PRINTED IN THE NETHERLANDS

Contents

	PREFACE	vii
I	INTRODUCTION	1
II	REASON AND IMAGINATION	8
III	LANGUAGE GAMES AND LINGUISTIC IMAGINATION	27
IV	METAPHOR AND MEANING	45
V	METAPHOR AND PHILOSOPHICAL DISCOURSE	62
VI	SUBVERSION AND INTENTION	79
VII	PHILOSOPHY AND POETRY	97
VIII	THE MYTH OF DESCRIPTION	117
IX	EPILOGUE	132
	INDEX	137

To
AMALA

Who was always interested in
what it was all about

Preface

If a Preface is intended to let the reader down more gently than an Introduction can, and give inside information not very explicit in the text, some explanatory remarks may be in order here. Engaged as I am in two different kinds of writing, philosophy and poetry, I am, as a matter of day-to-day experience, familiar with reflecting on the kind of craftsmanship needed in each. A good deal of figurative language enters into philosophical prose and plays an integral role in argument. Once this is recognised it seems to me that we can no longer regard philosophising as a purely conceptual exercise. The figurative language used by philosophers of the linguistic analytic persuasion is particularly illuminating in this regard, for among contemporary philosophers it is they who believe philosophy to be exclusively concerned with what they call 'concepts'.

Literary criticism links up figurative language with the functioning of the imagination, and justly so. The discredit associated with the 'poetic' in the minds of some philosophers is tied up with a misidentification of the imaginative and innovative with the imaginary and the fictional. If the record is set straight the way is clear for rehabilitating a conception of reason which is no longer denuded of imaginative power, and for appreciating the wealth rather than the limits of our linguistic resources, what view we take of reason and how we see language, being, in my opinion, closely related.

Along the way some hard things are said about contemporary philosophical obsessions with the banal and the commonplace. These are said more in sorrow than in anger. Much of contemporary literature bears a similar stamp. We owe to those in the analytic camp an awakening of interest in language. But we have still a long way to go in our sensitivity to the nuances of language. Not merely the corpus of everyday uses of language, but the entire range of literature of every culture is there before us as evidence of what can be said and has been said. Description, re-description, or even multi-description, are small areas within this limitless territory.

My focus has been on the language of metaphysics. But since both philosophers who are avowedly metaphysical and those who are avowedly anti-metaphysical use language in highly innovative ways my title remains 'The Language of Philosophy'. The main purport of what I have to say is not affected by the consideration that there are extensive stretches of philosophical discourse where logic is the chief key. To dwell on this would have been to labour the obvious.

If we compare what the metaphysician does with what other writers do it is with the poet that we find ourselves chiefly engaged. The language of ethics and of religion would come in for scrutiny, I have no doubt, in association with the analysis of drama and of the novel, and I am very conscious of having neglected the intimate relation between metaphysics and ethics, seen paradigmatically in the work of Plato.

Above all I have tried to explore the *momentum* of metaphysical thought, how we feel our way, rather than to delineate the destinations we may or may not reach. To see linguistic imagination at work in encouraging this momentum situates philosophy importantly in the humanities in a way which seems to me sadly needed. The philosopher, like the artist in words, has language as his medium. His natural confreres are not scientists and technicians, but *other writers*. The dichotomy between interpreting and changing the world is a false one. Men like Karl Marx and John Dewey brought about changes through the very vehicle of their writing. Powerful writing, whether it be that of Plato or Marx, Aquinas or Heidegger, never leaves things exactly as they were because they do not leave *us* as we were.

I have not scrupled to draw on the armouries of both the analyst and the phenomenologist. It has also been found necessary to move back and forth in time. I offer no apology for this for I believe that to think metaphysically is to engage in strenuous dialogue with the thinkers of the past. The very language we inherit is shaped by the writings they have left behind. And among these thinkers none are more *present*, for those with a natural disposition towards metaphysics, than Plato and Kant.

I must mention that I owe much to Friedrich Waismann, my former teacher, whose work contains many insights which chime in with much of what I have tried to explore in this book, although it is only fair to grant that there are probably as many features of his thinking which pull in an opposite direction. If anything else needs mentioning it is perhaps this – my involvement with music, as performer and critic, and the circumstance that I need to operate with several languages in my daily existence. These are in no way extraordinary matters, and the reader will have no difficulty in detecting how they enter into my attempts at philosophising.

MARGARET CHATTERJEE
"Rokeby"
Landour
Mussoorie, India.
June 1979

" 'Tis not solely in poetry and music we must follow our taste and sentiment, but likewise in philosophy."

> (David Hume, *A Treatise of Human Nature*, Book I, Pt. III, Sec. VIII.)

"...when the sense of mystery and enchantment no longer draws the mind to wander aimlessly, and to love it knows not what: when, in short, twilight has no charm – then metaphysics will be worthless."

> (F.H. Bradley, *Appearance and Reality*, pp. 3-4.)

"Metaphysicians, like artists, are the antennae of the time: they have a flair for feeling which way the spirit is moving."

> (F. Waismann, *How I See Philosophy*, p. 38.)

CHAPTER I

Introduction

The theme which underlies this book is the nature of philosophical language and philosophical thinking. Is there such a thing as philosophical prose? Can it be taken for granted that it is the philosopher's business to eschew poetry? Socrates advised Glaucon to polish his concepts and perhaps the major thrust of philosophical thought in ancient Greece took it for granted that the attainment of the concept was the central redoubt of all philosophic endeavour. Even if the goal was reached via the highly-coloured terrain of myth and allegory the goal itself was a shining lucidity, an intelligibility which had left behind picutre-making. That much in Plato's own make-up and his craft of writing pulled in other directions is well known. As long as mathematics and logic provide the main models for the philosopher, the role of imagery is understandably underplayed. But the models of the natural sciences have crippled philosophy no less. Taking the cue from the 'stoppers' of the verificatory process the positivists held up as a model the idea of literality. Even those who abandoned the basic proposition *ignis fatuus* still retained a fixation on particularity and on a kind of description where we would be brought up short by 'the facts'. The distinction between 'ordinary' and technical language obscured the fact that ordinary language is not ordinary at all and that, even if it were, it ill becomes the philosopher to succumb to the oracles of the market-place.

In certain circles, to do philosophy in any other way than the fashionable analytic way was to allow oneself to be bewitched by language (the crowning sin of an earlier generation was allowing oneself to be led astray by subject/predicate logic). At the same time, illogically enough, we were told that 'using' pictures in our thinking was inevitable, and were invited by the guru-figures to use a few more, like 'language games' and so on. The category shifts which had been the philosopher's stock-in-trade for centuries now suddenly became 'mistakes'. Only one man among the analysts, a much neglected figure, Friedrich Waismann, saw the full implications of the polymorphic approach to language. Philosophy, he wrote, "as it is practised today, is very unlike science".[1] This was plain speaking for those who imagined they were doing philosophy in a scientific manner par excellence. He was writing from within the analytic tradition when he went on to refer to the philosopher as "a man

---

[1] *How I see Philosophy*, F. Waismann, Macmillan, 1968, p. 1.

who senses as it were hidden crevices in the build of our concepts where others only see the smooth path of commonplaceness before them".[2] But he by no means advocated the return to the commonplace as a way out. In fact "a departure from the beaten track...may be the *very thing* to be striven for – in poetry, science and in philosophy".[3]

In the meantime those who were pedagogically concerned with philosophy (no one with any respect for Socrates and his method would regard it as a compliment to be called a 'professional philosopher') were keen to compare philosophy with science or with religion but never with poetry. It was taken for granted that poetry was as far from philosophy as you could get. Yet both were traditionally supposed to be concerned with truth, and both are currently relegated by analysts to a no man's land where truth and falsity do not obtain. Both busy themselves with meaning, and both set great store by meticulous expression. If it were not for Richards' sweeping distinction between the emotive and the referential maybe the common concerns of poets and philosophers would have become evident, for heaven knows there was no simple referent for what the analysts wanted to say.[4] The common ground remained unrecognised – the common invitation of poet and philosopher to the reader to look at the world in a new way. It was not an appeal the *analytic* philosopher in any case could make because of his insistence on leaving things as they were. This itself was a confession of bankruptcy. For when things are said well they never leave things exactly as they are. When things are said well they do not lead us to stoppers, even to the stoppers of actual usage, but lend thought and imagination wings and can even lead to action. For common sense, as Funke neatly put it, is not the avant-garde of philosophic thought but its arrière-garde.

Is there such a thing as philosophical language or poetic language? The former, again traditionally, is taken to be discourse, that is reasoned argument. This is illustrated by a contemporary writer, Bernard Williams, who lays stress on argumentation as integral to philosophy in his recent work on Descartes: "The incapacity to tell the difference between the power of words and the force of argument (prevalent, then as now, in Paris) contributed to the sceptical disorientation which existed in Descartes' time."[5] But the history of philosophy is not hospitable to any such sharp distinction. No great writer of philosophic prose, be he Plato or Bradley, has been deaf to the power of words. And it has been their sensitivity to the 'powers' of words that has lent content and force to their arguments. Another unsatisfactory demarcation is made by Toulmin in a

---

[2]*Ibid.*, p. 2.
[3]*Ibid.*, p. 175.
[4]The impact of Richards' distinction is shown in Carnap's denigrating statement that "metaphysical propositions – like lyrical verses – have only an expressive function, but no representative function". *Philosophy and Logical Syntax*, Eng. trans., London, 1935, p. 28.
[5]*Descartes : The Project of Pure Enquiry*, Penguin, 1978.

INTRODUCTION

recent work[6] where he writes, "Literature and the fine arts occupy an interesting position: halfway between the fully-disciplined enquiries of physical science, on the one hand, and such non-disciplinable fields as ethics and philosophy on the other." Only someone quite unengaged in the craft of literature could assign such a place to it. The quotation, however, is otherwise interesting in the way philosophy is kept apart from the natural sciences, following presumably in the line of post-Wittgensteinian philosophers like Lazerowitz who are committed to this demarcation owing to their view that philosophical statements are neither true nor false. The power of words is seen in a vivid way in metaphor. We shall see the extent to which philosophical prose utilises metaphor and along with this how the philosophic metaphor compares with the poetic metaphor. This will serve not only to focus on a neglected aspect of many philosophical arguments (their dependence on metaphor) but enable us to confront the bogey of approximation to poetry. The point is not, for example, could Bergson have said what he wanted to say in any other way, but what *did* he say. If recent work suggests that the phrase 'philosophical language' may be out of date, no less is this the case with the phrase 'poetic language'. The distance between them thereby narrows, but not that there is any possibility, let alone fear, of their approximating to each other. Rather those who wish to make a point, whether in philosophy or in poetry, need to do it skilfully.

The use of figurative language by some of the analytic philosophers themselves repays examination, for it opens up the whole question of the legitimacy of category-shifts. Our thinking after all is not only bewitched by language but rather made possible by it and enriched by its resources.[7] It is only in fact by having an ear for the resources of language, including its resonances, that our insights can attain articulate formulation. The transfers of vocabulary that we make are admittedly fraught with danger, simply because they operate outside the range of 'rules'. It is ironical that one of the leading examples, that of the concept of language-game (intended to point up the linkage of linguistic usage and rules) should prove highly misleading. The 'stratum' analogy suggested by Waismann provides an alternative model, a hierarchical classificatory one, which deserves close attention.

But the study of metaphors and language-games remains on the operational level. Another way of proceeding is to explore the noetic sources of meaning in the capacities of the human psyche. This leads to the sort of enquiry which above all Dilthey thought most crucial. Beyond the demarcations of faculty psychology there is a matrix which those engaged in the study of all man's symbolic activities are alive to. To say, however, that philosophy and poetry

---

[6]*Human Understanding*, S. Toulmin, (Princeton University Press, Cambridge University Press), Vol. I, 1972, p. 396.

[7]Richards spoke of the 'resourcefulness' of words and yet had a very narrow conception of the 'resources' of language.

are creative activities is not enough. We need to probe what makes them different from each other. Hinterland and context[8] are operative in each, that is to say, in brief, psychical determinants and situational matrices are both shaping agencies. But do these factors affect validity or not? The thrust of Lazerowitz' rejection of the true/false dichotomy with regard to philosophic statements stems from his assessment and weightage of the hinterland factor. The Marxist appreciation of the contextual is naturally geared to cultural and historical relativism. But this does not mean that a *darshana* cannot be a valid perspective or a perspective that others cannot share. In today's world of intercultural sharing the idiosyncrasy of a particular perspective need not make it opaque to someone who subscribes to another perspective. Even if we cannot but see through our own spectacles, something of the contours which others also see will emerge in our field of vision. What *is* ruled out, however, is the idea that events and circumstances are so *opaque* as to make them only the *terminus* of enquiries. Such an idea means the death of both philosophy and poetry. For both, particulars are the *point de départ*, the stimulus to inquiry and insight, rather than the building bricks of an edifice.

There is, then, some point in contemporary caveats in certain circles that philosophy is divergent from science, despite a host of efforts to make it otherwise from Aristotle, through to Descartes, Kant and Russell. To find that philosophy is more like the arts than the sciences should not occasion surprise, for man is *homo faber*, and philosophy and poetry both involve doing and making. Neither the philosopher nor the artist leaves things (nor us ourselves) as they are. A Plato, a Berkeley or a Bergson alters our perspective no less radically than does a Cézanne. To remain at the merely verbal level is therefore to abdicate from the vocation of the philosopher, and small wonder that the man-in-the-street never comes to hear the names of such practitioners. If the world were the totality of facts there would be no room for philosophers and poets in it.

There is, it seems, a real sense in which an understanding of the role of philosophy and poetry ties in with an understanding of what man himself is like. Both philosophy and poetry belong to the noösphere, to borrow Teilhard de Chardin's term. The noösphere, no doubt, cannot *survive* without the spheres which sustain life. When these very spheres are threatened, whether through scarcity, one-dimensionality, warfare or other causes the noösphere itself comes under threat. When horizons shrink, attempts are made to define philosophy so as to make it a part of the natural world. But this can only be done by abrogating the task of philosophy. Both the philosopher and the poet begin with *vāk*, with speech. Both engage in transcending acts which extend the horizons of experience. The vocations of both grew out of a matrix in which early man experimented with sounds and found he could build structures not made by hands. These were not aery nothings, but powerful symbol-systems

---

[8]Vide my book *Our Knowledge of Other Selves* for a discussion of these terms.

which shaped his day-to-day living. What Marx pleaded for was for something which *had* obtained in early history, when the word was powerful and enabled men to change reality. It would be a thousand pities for the philosopher to acquiesce in a world which is a totality of facts, or fail to see in the quest for vision, or clarification of insight a task very akin to the poet's and in the course of which he of necessity does in fact draw very considerably on the armoury of the poet.

Now central to the analytic philosopher's goal of producing aseptic clear and distinct prose is the belief that it is the philosopher's business to 'describe' and that this should not involve the imagination. Above all 'fantasy' is to be eschewed. The analytic philosopher, therefore, takes pride in dealing with 'concepts' of this and that, with boundaries, demarcations, identifications, rules and the like, in fact he shows his allegiance to a programme which is fully rationalistic. The only difference is that instead of the *a priori* we are offered 'what in fact is the case'. This is dressed up in as inexorable a manner as the law of the Medes and the Persians, throwing to the winds the message of Lewis Carroll's Alice who saw so clearly that words mean just what we decide they shall mean.

Looking at the history of philosophy we find that the incorporation of imagination into veridical perception by Hume confirmed Plato's association of *eikasis* with the 'sensitive' part of our nature. This important insight, as far as perception was concerned, was not for nothing in Hume combined with a rejection of speculation in any form in philosophy. The underlying reason, however, was hidden from Hume, that thinking devoid of imagination is not *capable* of the speculative impulse. For Hume, imagination is an aid, an indispensable aid, to the perception of particulars. Its work, in other words, is subordinate to the discovery of termini for inquiry, a discovery that depends on the filling in of gap-indifferent series of ideas by the imagination. This in itself was an important advance over the view which saw imagination only as a source of the non-veridical. It took centuries of research in psychology, experience of the extension of sensibility through drugs etc. to shake the view that the senses as such can serve as a terminus ad quem. The role of imagination in religious thought, or its place in mathematical research (something stressed by Hardie) all went disregarded. Particularity remained the model, even as far as Strawson, a particularity identified by something uncommonly like what earlier generations of realists called acquaintance. Now although it was no doubt necessary, in order to make sense of our cognitive endeavours, to be able to say that we do on *some* occasions know, there was no need to throw overboard the lessons of Hume and Kant, various as these were; in the one case recognising the supplementary task of empirical imagination, and in the other, the indispensability of categorical frameworks. It all depends on whether inquiry is to *terminate* with the discovery of the data or *begin* precisely there. The building bricks model which started in the seventeenth century died with Hume and Kant. And yet linguistic polymorphism was unable to move sufficiently far away from the influence of a simplified understanding of empiricality which was still insufficiently liberated from thinking in terms of units on the analogy of the chemical sciences. Such a simplified understanding closes the door to seeing particularity as a *point de départ*, a clue for a conspectus which is not aimed at the discovery of law, or more and more facts, but at the discovery of meaning, a speculum mentis which is not very unlike what the poet seeks and to which the work of the imagination is absolutely integral. To see eternity in a grain of sand is not to see the grain as a terminal point, nor as the instantiation of a law, but as an expression of a *universality* which has little to do with the categories of logic. It is of the same order as the universality Hardy sees in the old man turning the clods.

Resistance to the idea that reason and imagination can no longer be kept in separate compartments is fed from yet another source. There is a fear in certain quarters that the work of the unmaskers, namely Darwin, Nietzsche, Marx and Freud, threatens the very credentials of thought. But why need such unmasking be looked upon as a threat? Man bears incapsulated within himself his whole heritage, his past, his history, and his present stretches into the future in action, hope and thought. To see this 'environing' of his being in terms of 'determining', or of coordinates, is to commit the error of reductionism. The time dimensions of man's existence not only situate man in Being in a sense which builds temporality into the very nature of Being, but bring out the centrality of imagination to his own being, for it is only in imagination (through memory) that he belongs to the past and through projection that he also belongs to the future. It is language that enables us to bring to the forefront of consciousness what lay in the past and what might be in the future. To understand this, however, requires an understanding of the way that imagination operates in our linguistic activities. To begin with, we see that language is not merely a matter of operating with counters. At first it was the operators which attracted philosophers' attention, words like 'if', 'but' and the like. This, in itself, was an advance on the earlier name-centred philosophy of language which Ogden and Richards exposed critically in their book *The Meaning of Meaning*. Yet norms and operators are but elements in the rich texture which language has. The leverage is "what one wants to say". The very leverage is intentional, a reaching out, of which the desire to know is *one* type. There can be no going back on Kant's exclusion of metaphysics from *scientific knowledge*. But knowledge does not exhaust man's noetic activities. The old classification of belief and opinion along with the cognitive activities was sound. But metaphysical thinking provides an example of yet another kind of activity the nature of which we have yet to examine.

A notable element in the present impasse about the nature of metaphysics, and the lack of sympathy in certain quarters for what used to be called the speculative impulse, arises, surprising though this may seem, from the emancipation of philosophical thought from theological concern. This emancipation, for which Kant was in no small part responsible, has been taken to be a symptom of advance. But from another point of view it is the philosopher who has been thereby impoverished. To see the close involvement of faith and imagination has been the key insight of men like Richard Kroner. But to see the two as mutually involved was further to discredit imagination in the eyes of the tough-minded. For imagination to be grounded in sensibility was bad enough, but for it to be directed towards the supersensible seemed folly par excellence. In so dismissing the question, the empiricist (for this is the camp to which such a line of attack belongs) is led astray by the polar opposition between sensible and super-sensible (or non-sensible), forgetting that the sensible is also counterposed to, say, natural law, to history and to that of which we have dim intimation; that these are neither super-sensible nor a priori but that each has a separate status of its own, and that to none of these is the working of imagination foreign. I include here the scientific imagination out of which models and theories are born, the historical imagination which embraces period and style no less than event and idea, and the 'fringe', the 'ragged edges' of disciplines, which are less limit than frontier of the new, 'bounding' on possibility. Ironically the separation of philosophy from theology struck at the very credentials of reason, for in losing its fons et origo, its link with divinity, it suffered a loss of pedigree from which it has never recovered. This is a separate but nonetheless relevant story.

We mentioned the rationalist bias of the analytic philosopher. Has it not been a fashion to set false limits to reason's powers? The composer and the poet are indeed surprised to find that reason is regarded as the self-confessed preserve of the mathematician, the logician and the philosopher. Indeed one of the chief things that is at stake in an analysis of philosophical language is the whole question of the reach of reason. Historically the resources of the term 'reason' are rich and diverse. It is easiest here to think in dichotomies, the sensible and the intellective, the intuitive and the discursive. It is less easy, but it may be wiser, to build into 'ratio' much that we had learnt to exclude from it. We may be urged to do so if we take the findings of the psycho-analysts seriously, and refuse to be bullied into seeing this as in any way undermining the pedigree of thought. There can be no outreach without a base and without movement from that base. The creative ventures of the human mind of which philosophy and poetry are highly articulated and condensed expressions, are fed from man's total psychic resources. To see it otherwise is to impoverish these ventures and with no justifiable warrant. Only by rediscovering these resources can the role of philosophy as something unashamedly non-scientific be affirmed and vindicated. But first we need to see how philosophers have actually used language in the past, and the extent to which this is correlated with how they regard reason and imagination.

CHAPTER II

Reason and Imagination

To look at the history of philosophy with an eye to the kind of language used is perhaps unusual. No doubt along with this one needs to examine the structure of arguments and the directions in which reasoning leads. Even the most lucid of philosophical writers find it difficult to keep up the standard of linearity which rational discourse seems to require. The perspective of insight leads across gaps, calls upon cross references and invites us to seek a kinship among apparent dissimilarities. Meanings cluster round a centre, disperse, lead in new directions, fanning out towards new horizons. To form a concept within the flux that living thought is, is very evidently a task fraught with difficulty. But it is a task which Greek philosophers, above all, thought to be eminently worthwhile. So it came about that the concept came to be regarded as a triumphant conquest, the carving of boundedness out of chaos, the imposition of order on anarchy. Since such an attitude dies hard, even after centuries, it is well to look further into it.

Speculative thought grew out of a mythological matrix, behind Plato standing the powerful figures of Homer and Hesiod. Cornford finds in fifth-century Athens a milieu where "profound and far-reaching thoughts had been released to hover, as it were in a disembodied state, and haunt the minds of men who could not capture more than a fragment of their meaning in the precision of a formula".[1] And he speaks of Empedocles' philosophy as "animated and illuminated from within by this poetic gift of insight, though here as elsewhere, the Muses may sometimes be telling a false tale that is only like the truth". What is the relation between mythopoeic thinking and the more abstract thinking of the philosopher? Psycho-analyst Carl Jung maintains that "philosophy is internally nothing else but a refined and sublimated mythology". Without using the clinical language of sublimation, Peter Munz comes close to this view by saying that metaphysical propositions "are the conceptual summaries of myths". Now if the myth be an extended metaphor, a metaphor expanded into a narrative, myth itself can be said to have a certain linearity, the linearity of 'the story'. But this would be far too narrow an understanding of myth, for the mythopoeic provides a milieu in which men *live*. It is this living matrix which the philosopher who draws on myth is fed by. But the

---

[1]*From Religion to Philosophy*, p. ix.

ambivalence of the philosopher's attitude to myth becomes clear at this point, because his thought draws on what eventually he aspires to leave behind. The aspiration of reason to formulate the concept is itself shaped by the matrix which gives it birth. The totality of Plato's vision, his rooting in the literary tradition of his own culture, enables him to recognise this, although for other reasons, especially his pedagogic concern with *paideia*, he is critical of *poets* rather than of the poetic impulse itself. In the *Ion* for example, the point is made that since poets are stimulated by a non-rational inspiration they can hardly be competent guides for the conduct of life. Kant, on the other hand, taking the natural sciences as a model, can find in the excursions of pure reason only a beating of wings in empty space. A post-Freudian generation may agree, but for non-Kantian reasons. Pure reason, shorn of all connections with the psyche, is an impoverished faculty indeed.

As a pupil of Socrates, Plato was inclined to deprecate the role of myths, to regard them as mere play, for in the *Phaedrus* Socrates speaks plainly, referring to the interpretation of myths as "this bootless wisdom". It is in the same dialogue, however, that Socrates himself uses an extended metaphor, saying to Phaedrus: "...But noble far is the serious pastime of the dialectician who, finding a congenial soul, by the help of science sows and plants therein words which are able to defend themselves and him who planted them, and are not unfruitful, but have in them a seed which others brought up in different soils render immortal, making the possessors of it happy to the utmost extent of human happiness."[2] His point is that writing is inferior to speech. Those familiar with Manu's use of the seed/soil analogy may wonder if Socrates attached equal importance to seed and soil. And of course the seed of the word idea was used with other connotations in the Patristic period of church history. Socrates did not inveigh against the poets, but saved his criticisms for the Sophists whom he castigated not for flights of imagination but for their reduction of philosophy to a play upon and with words.

It would be rash, perhaps, to try to isolate Socratic influence from Plato's own view about language. But occasionally a sentence rings out as specially born of Plato's own thinking. In the *Cratylus*, for example, he warns us that "if we are over-precise about words, truth will say 'too late' to us as to the belated traveller in Aegina".[3] It is in the *Cratylus*, moreover, that Plato gives a telling answer to those, in his day or ours, who identify the rationale of language with mere usage. Language is an instrument of *thought* and can express thought accurately. The satire on Prodicus in the *Protagoras* shows how Plato regards attempts to confine the meaning of words. In the *Ion, Apology* and *Meno* he hints at a faculty in men which cannot be reduced to rule and measure, something which could be called inspiration, imagination or even aspiration. How else otherwise to account for the very nerve of the ascent of reason itself? If "words

[2]*Phaedrus*, 276C.
[3]*Cratylus*, 433e.

are more plastic than wax",[4] this is not a cause of regret. There can be no doubt about the philosophical profitability of Plato's use of figurative speech. In fact in the *Gorgias, Phaedo* and *Phaedrus* we have a portrait of the soul's nature and destiny which has an undoubted literary quality. One can see, in Plato, philosophy taking the place of epic poetry as the cradle of ethics, politics and almost everything else. At the same time Plato was concerned to stress the *specialist* character of the philosopher's task. If the world of Forms is to take the place of Olympus how does this affect the role of the philosopher as a writer? Plato grapples with this question in the *Republic*, especially in his criticisms of poet and poetry in Book X to which we must now turn.

There seem to have been two main charges, that poetical or artistic creations give us only shadows or reflexions of things, and that poetry fosters the growth of passions. The former point arises from his belief that poetic imagination was unaided by "the calculating or the reasoning element in the soul". From this it follows that poetry is "far from the truth", it does not imitate it, it is produced without knowledge of the truth and it does not "lay hold on truth". The point about imitation needs some scrutiny. We usually think that Plato was hostile to poetry on the ground that poetry deals with *mimesis* and therefore distracts men from dwelling on the one that stands over against the many. If this were so, the argument would not be convincing for in *Republic* 598B he makes the point that poetry "does not imitate the truth". Even if poetry did work through *mimesis* this would not have constituted an argument against it, for *mimesis* is one of Plato's own doctrines regarding the relation of the particular and the universal. His own ontology would allow that an in-depth awareness of the particular (such as for example one finds in a certain kind of poetry) could provide entry to the universal. Objections on moral grounds therefore may be more cogent.

The point about raising passions stems from the exemplars provided in the stories of Homer and Hesiod which were reckoned to have an undesirable influence. We would need a further assumption here, that the general run of men are actually *affected* by what epic writers write. How are we to surmise an answer to this? The modern writer today would be flattered at the idea that his products actually affect the way the populace might behave. In an Indian context, Ram, the epic hero, is regarded as an ideal, and yet could one say that the behaviour of ordinary people was in any way modelled on the behaviour of Ram? One can only conclude that Plato regarded the portrayal of exemplars as immensely important and that he thought this should not be left to the writers of epics. Granted that the behaviour of the denizens of Mt. Olympus was often far from edifying, Plato's attitude here, as so often elsewhere, is shaped by his overriding concern as a moralist. But even so, how are we to square all this with the words of the *Phaedrus*, that "the soul which has seen most of truth shall come to the birth as a philosopher, or artist, or some

---

[4]*Republic*, 588d.

musical and loving nature". This would suggest that the philosopher is a supreme artist in his knowledge of essences. In order to expand the path of dialectical reason it is perfectly admissible to use symbols, allegories and myths. This is to say, even though poetry is 'untrue', a poet can write 'noble lies' and a philosopher is free to use poetic language where linear discourse does not suffer. In his unpublished *Fragments* he went even further, hinting that poetry could take us beyond the reach of dialectical reason. *Noesis* as vision, or sublime intuition, lent itself to such an interpretation although Plato must have seen the crowning paradox of the poet's craft, the attempt to symbolise the unsymbolisable.

But we are not yet in the clear, because the foregoing argument would seem to pull in the opposite direction from the main thrust of the Divided Line analogy, where the ascent of reason is seen above all as a flight from all that is sensible or a semblance of the sensible. If the soul bears within itself the fruit of its past experience this would provide a clue to the 'informing' of reason by the whole journey of its ascent, a process breaking forth in the inspired flights which a later generation associated with 'imagination' but which are far indeed from *eikasis*, the lowest rung of the noetic scale, flights which are the special gifts of both philosopher and poet. If this were so it would account for the undoubted 'poetic' content in Plato's own thought, but given his veneration of Socrates, it would also account for a lingering sense that the *purely intelligible* would be still yet *beyond* that, a surmise which is certainly strengthened by the sun analogy.

In Raphael's fresco of the School of Athens in the Vatican, Plato is shown pointing upward to the heavens while Aristotle points earthward down a flight of steps. Whether or not this be altogether just or not is a matter of opinion. But few would deny Aristotle's concern with the concrete. Without the ontology of natural kinds, perception of similitude would not be possible, and without this there could be neither *definitions* nor the use of metaphor for ornamentation in rhetoric. It is important to remember that attempts to create an 'art of discourse' were concerned with the spoken word, that is, with oratory, for it is the orator who learns most about the power of words. The discussion of rhetoric thus not unnaturally became tied up more with questions of morality than of metaphysics. Gorgias had maintained that an orator could argue a just and an unjust cause with equal effectiveness. It is in the context of discussing style and how a speech should be constructed that Aristotle comes to talk of metaphors and figures of speech in his *Rhetoric*. Rhetorical training as taught by the Sophists had come under fire by Socrates. But there were those who maintained that rhetoric was, or at least could be, highly moral since truth and justice offered the best occasions for persuasion. Although Book III of the *Rhetoric* deals with literary style, Aristotle has far more to say about literature in the *Poetics*. For Aristotle, as for Plato, the principle which activates poetic activity (which is one of the productive activities) is *mimesis*.

This, together with his classificatory bias, makes Aristotle's own philosophical style tilt sharply in favour of a scientific approach, an approach which we find in fact is one of the most influential streams in the history of western philosophy.

Twentieth-century concern with sentence structure is the most recent development of the Greek concern with frameworks. The Greek was fascinated by the limitless, but tended to identify it with chaos, even with the barbarians that lived beyond the islands that hugged the coast. The bounded figures of geometry, the temple precincts that house gods – in their very limits set a norm of intelligibility. Mythological spaces and time, heroes with unpredictable fortunes – all these were the reverse of the chiselled concept, the figures which emerge from the rock under the master hand of the sculptor. Of all the arts perhaps sculpture served as the most positive model for the philosopher. Cutting, chiselling and polishing required hard labour, and the result had a permanence and fixity which was at the opposite pole from the ephemeral impact of the spoken word.

Yet in its most imaginative reaches Greek philosophy was poetic and Greek poetry (drama) was philosophic. Greek philosophy set the stage for two major trends in the history of western philosophy, the one an aspiration towards the scientific, and the other the sense that it would be in no way an advantage to philosophy for it to emulate the sciences. Plato, one might say, fathered both tendencies. Aristotle belongs squarely in the scientific tradition. And yet we owe to Aristotle, at least by implication, an insight which all too often gets lost in discussions on literature by those who are not actually engaged in the craft themselves. Aristotle's analysis of poetry and drama, whether or not contemporary practice has thrown all his canons aside, shows clearly that literature is far from mere dithyramb. Art involves conceptual thinking in a high degree. If this be so we do wrong to stress the intuitive character of art versus the intellective character of philosophy. Both philosophy and poetry struggle with the inarticulate, striving to make it articulate. Each strives for the attainment of 'fittingness'. When articulated fully, the deliverances of each cannot be put any other way.

All the great rationalists from Plato onwards saw that man was imperfectly rational. This was reflected perhaps more in man's behaviour than in his thought, although this is not a distinction which Socrates and Plato would take kindly to. The kind of penetrative intellect which complete rationality might involve would be intuitive rather than discursive, for both Plato and Spinoza. But it was not *unlike* the kind of glimpse which, at least momentarily, the poet might have access to. That is to say, the twilight world which imperfect reason is familiar with is occasionally shot through with an intelligibility which yields itself up to the poetic impulse. How different really were the kinds of conspectus, of vision, open to the philosopher and the poet? In each case we had a partial intelligibility, which to the theist was further illumined by revelation.

Mediaeval thought, for all its insistence on the work of reason as an indispensable preamble to faith and its belief in the fortifying of reason by revelation, strengthened and widened the scope of reason and this is a way which has not always been given sufficient credit. The New Testament parables were regarded as vehicles of truth, reaching their audience through appeal to the familiar. So far from bordering on the apocalyptic imagery which was somewhat distrusted by orthodox Jewish thought, they were caught up as part of the very texture of the Word, the elucidation of which by argument aids our understanding of the *kerygma*. They provide a context which is highly relevant to the theologian's exploration of *analogia entis*, founded as that is on our familiarity with the day-to-day world. At the same time, for all the Aristotelian underpinnings of St. Thomas' *Summa*, there is something Platonic about the mediaeval schoolmen's metaphysic, namely, the view that one all-embracing focal vision can illuminate all the minutiae of human existence, for Plato, the vision of the Form of the Good, and, for the Christian, the vision of Christ crucified. But whereas for the Platonist it is a vision which would come as the climax of a recognised path in which the entire life of reason is engaged, for the Christian it comes as the intrusion of a *scandalon*, something for which the rest of his experience is hardly a preparation. In the latter case categorial discourse breaks down. But in each case we are eventually invited to see the familiar afresh in the light of the vision that has broken in on us. The Christian, unlike the Platonist, will not speak of the vision as 'unaided'. All man's physical resources could not batter against the opaque density of the empirical and find meaning in it were not the whole of creation shaped and ordered in a manner which went beyond facticity. But to say this is to give a warrant for the utter stretching of our faculties and our language, a move which the empiricist cannot conscience. It is one of the strange quirks of the history of philosophy that Kant, born into the rationalist tradition as he was, should have so deeply understood the empiricist frame of thought. But at the same time it is Kant in the modern period who best of all recognised the possibility of non-categorial thinking even though it would not result in knowledge. When Dilthey in one of his writings hints at the affinity of Kant with Plato rather than with Aristotle, he does this advisedly.

What Kant means by metaphysics is made clear in his *Schriften*[5] where he says "metaphysics is a science of delimiting human reason", and "it is useful in that it abolishes illusion which can be dangerous". The warnings Kant gives about transcendental illusion are echoed in many of Wittgenstein's obiter dicta, e.g. that "an analogy irresistably drags us on", we are not "able to rid ourselves of the implications of our symbolism", pictures "hold us captive", similes "produce false appearances", grammatical illusions are "deeply rooted in our experiences", we have an "urge to misunderstand", a "craving for generality and completeness". The points are strikingly similar. Kant was concerned

[5] XX, p. 181.

with the range of our concepts and Wittgenstein with the range of our linguistic expression. Herder, who was Kant's pupil in Koenigsberg during the seventeen sixties, wrote critically of Kant in his *Metakritik* on the ground that Kant omits the state of our language, considering only thought and the world. For both Hamann and Herder it is the living word of communication between man and man that is of interest. In this they are one with Socrates. But they saw man's symbolising activities, whether it be in religion, history, art or philosophy, as stemming from a matrix where intellect, will and emotion were not to be set apart from each other. Kant on the other hand held to the faculty psychology assumed by Wolff and his contemporaries according to which the natural preserve of philosophical activity must needs be the intellect. 'Intellect' was in fact the term used in the early works, before Kant hit upon the diverse functions of reason and understanding. In Herder's view the mistaken approach of faculty psychology distorts not only epistemology but politics, ethics, and art as well. To Herder, if nature is a unity of *Kräfte*, of powers, so also is man. The mere counters which words are, only come to life in communication. Hamann speaks of the valley of dry bones which only a Socrates, a St. Paul or a Luther, can cover with flesh. Herder uses very similar language in referring to the linguistic "petrifaction" against which men rightly revolt. This is to say more than to locate the important thing about language in use or usage. It is to highlight the importance of use and usages of a particular kind. In admiring Leibniz rather than Kant, Herder recognised, if not a champion of the indistinct and the unclear, at least one who saw no sharp line of demarcation between them on the one hand and the Cartesian certainties. Herder's message was that man could find himself by a rediscovery of the wellsprings within and "cease to be in contradiction with himself". A generation familiar with Freud can look at this rather more sympathetically than could those who were brought up to regard the romantics as all misguided.

To return to Kant, his prescription for the would-be metaphysician precluded admission of the role of imagination in metaphysical thinking, as, for him, both the categorial and the projective functions of mind were thought to be intellective. The blurring of boundaries between the sensitive and the cogitative was something that Kant made room for only in perception (the role given to imagination in the subjective deduction of the categories) and in aesthetic experience. And as for the 'hidden nature of man' what interested him most was what made of man a moral being. Kant would not share Windelband's assessment of German thought between 1780 and 1820, identifying its strength as lying "just in the league between philosophy and poetry".[6] Kant was always wary of *Schwärmerei*. He, however, was one with Goethe and Rousseau in seeing creativity as a species of human freedom. But this creativity was exemplified in the concreteness of moral actions and works

[6]*History of Philosophy*, p. 530.

of art and not in the speculative metaphysician's emulation of the dove soaring through the air unimpeded in its flight. Kant's teaching in the Dialectic opened new horizons, for it showed that there are mental activities other than pointing and proving. To say that the regulative function of the Ideas was at work on the categories of understanding was at least to *root* its excursions in the sphere of the knowable, wherever else the thrust of metaphysical thinking may take us. But the concepts which incite us to tear down all boundaries no longer serve as a reliable guide, for in their case thinking has lost its rule character. To 'beckon', as the Ideas do, is to give no guidance as to the steps to be taken in between.

Within the Kantian framework it is not hard to see why Kant is unable to see imagination (even the productive imagination) as cast for this guiding role. Imagination serves as a mediator between sense and understanding and therefore cannot serve as a mediator between understanding and reason. Herder had criticised Kant for neglecting analogy. The scholastic use of *analogia entis* is very evidently debarred to one committed to the transcendental method. Yet, Kant does use a considerable number of cosmological metaphors and analogies. But in treating of the 'Ideal of Reason' he warns us that "the products of imagination are of an entirely different nature" and the very word "Schattenbild" suggests the cave, a sphere hopelessly confined to shadows. In the *Prologomena*[7] Kant says that "...the imagination may perhaps be forgiven", but "the understanding which ought to think can never be forgiven for substituting extravagance; for we depend upon it alone for assistance to set bounds, when necessary to the extravagance of the imagination...."

And yet which faculty is more a source of extravagance, imagination or reason? Here we need to look at Kant's relation to perhaps the major figure in the romantic movement, Rousseau. It is common knowledge that when Rousseau's *Émile* first came into Kant's hands he was so absorbed in it that he gave up his daily walk. And this is what Rousseau wrote in that work: "One of the errors of our age is to use reason in too naked a form as if men were all mind....Reason alone is not active; she rarely restrains, she rarely excites, and she never has done anything great. To reason always is the mania of small minds."[8] The drawbacks of reason are conceived rather differently by Kant. They are twofold – the absence of empirical anchorage and the tendency to fall into antinomies. The link is clear. Without an empirical anchorage we have no ground for distinguishing between is and is not, hence we land in antinomies. Kant does not see the need for connecting imagination and reason any more than he finds any relation between imagination and will. In other words, he is concerned neither with the 'springs' of thought nor of action. Here too we can

[7] Paragraph 35.
[8] *Emile*, Complete Works. Ed. by V.D. Musset-Pathay, P. Dupont, Paris, 1823, III, pp. 134-7 (Fr. ed.).

see why. If the springs are regarded as totally empirical, that is, as contingent, they can never be the source of universality. The extent to which Kant identified the work of the mind with rules and procedures (finding even in genius a locus of rules) is no less than the way the devotees of linguistic analysis today concern themselves with uses and usages. The discussion has shifted from the conditions of cognition to the conditions of identification (which seems to be the current 'in' term). Strawson, after all, has written on Kant. The following quotation from Kant is interesting in this regard: "We are still far from the time," he writes in 1773, "when we can proceed synthetically in metaphysics; only when analysis has helped us to attain clear and explicitly understood concepts will synthesis be able to derive complicated cognitions from the simplest as in mathematics."[9] But the analysis which he completed years later was to close the door to any such "complicated cognitions". What he means by analysis must be remembered, i.e., beginning with what we actually have and exploring the conditions of its possibility. The work of productive imagination is given a rule character in the Schematism, but it is as cut off from Vernunft as the Platonic *eikasis* is from *noesis*. We are back, then, to a near-Platonic 'objection' to imagination, its lowly origins, in sensibility. Yet it is perhaps true to say that, for Kant, it is passions and emotions, and not imagination, that are the source of *Schwärmerei*. Kant was, to the last, a pupil of Newton; not the Newton who imaginatively conceives of the world as the sensorium of God, but the Newton for whom the universe exists in a fixed frame of reference. Heuristic principles may be unavoidable, but we need to avoid the mistake of regarding them as in any way related to the quest of the apodeictic. When Goethe spoke of his "poetic gifts" or his "common sense" stopping him from entering far into Kant's way of thinking[10] he voiced his general departure from Newtonian physics. It was not until he read the *Critique of Judgement* that he could feel that he found in Kant a kindred spirit.

We come to a different conclusion if we say that instead of reason being delimited it needs to be aided, that thought in fact needs wings. Hegel's recognition of the 'mobility' of living notions, their suggestive fringes, their directions, the new equilibria that constantly come about as they encounter each other, the shock that ripples out from a new example, the implications of an unusual metaphor, the way one notion can shade into another, the kaleidoscopic shifts which can set off trains of argument – all these make us think afresh about the momentum of thought. Once this momentum is granted we are in territory very like the one the poet inhabits, for the process of 'connecting' in each is akin. We have left definitions behind and are in a sea of thought where new horizons open on all sides. But all this means finding in teleology not merely a heuristic principle but the very nerve of thought itself.

[9] *Enquiry into the Evidences of the Principles of Natural Theology and Morals*, Werke, II, 191.
[10] "Einwirkung der neueren Philosophie", *Naturwissenschäftliche Schriften* (Weimar ed.) II, Abteilung, Bk. XI, 49.

When we turn to Hegel we find that for him imaginative, pictorial representation, falls short of the pure universality of conceptual thought. It is for this reason that he regards the imaginative presentations of religious consciousness as falling short of philosophy, for in the religious view otherness is not fully overcome. For particularity to bear the mark of the universal as it does, say, in the poetic image, is not enough. Self-conscious spirit will be able to articulate itself in concepts of its own. In the third section of his *Encyclopaedia, The Philosophy of Spirit,* however, Hegel has rather more to say about imagination, suggesting that the mind has a certain power over its pictorial representations, using them in a non-associatory manner, as symbolic vehicles of universal meaning. The role of imagination, therefore, has an indispensable role in that fusion of Word, Thing, and Notion that he understood by "true thought". The finding of the 'mot juste' was far from being a felicitous manipulation of counters. The treatment of poetry too is relevant here, for whereas the other arts 'remould' sensuous reality (painting, sculpture etc.) poetry, he says, "is not bound for its realization to external sensuous material", but "merely proceeds in the interior Space and Time of picture-thoughts and sensations".[11] And yet poetry, to Hegel, does not express the Idea fully. As for the complete Idea to which philosophy aspires, all our efforts in articulation are somehow internal to it. This in itself would mean that poetry and philosophy are by no means polar opposites. It is this reaching out, and yet without a sense of overstepping frontiers, which is the nerve of poetry and philosophy. It is precisely this reaching out which cannot be countenanced by those who think in terms of fixed tables of categories, of "limits of language".

Thought, for Hegel, is not teleological in any literal sense, that is, it does not move towards a fixed *telos* or end. But it is impelled by the very richness and diversity of the content which sets it in motion, nothing less than the depth and range of experience itself. And yet Hegel does not pass from art straight to philosophy, akin though poetry and philosophy may be. The transition to philosophy comes through an intermediate mode, that of religion. Hegel is strangely one with some of the contemporary analysts in identifying the religious with 'picture-using'. The idea of the Creator-God, for example, is an example of an 'imaginative concept' used by the theist. We shall see later that such concepts are used no less by the philosopher, and that the analyst's 'language-games' etc. have no less pictorial a function. So it comes about that both mythologisers and demythologisers, whether in theology or philosophy, find themselves bound to employ what Hegel called *Vorstellungen.* Now the Hegelian *Vorstellung* or imaginative concept is marked by its absence of rule character. It is a different *kind* of speculative instrument. But we would miss an important source of the momentum of thought if we were to ignore it. Even if we grant the role of *Vorstellungen* in both poetry and philosophy, there would, for Hegel, be no confusion between the two, for philosophy has as its task a

[11] *Lectures on Aesthetics,* I, p. 131.

reconstruction of the work of absolute reason through a process of reflection, something which no one would claim was the business of poetry. The impression, however, remained in certain circles, that German idealism and romanticism were interconnected and that this reflected discredit on the former. To this charge we must now turn.

Mainstream western thought up to the time of Kant had looked upon reason as penetrative rather than productive. The revolution which Kant's critical method introduced was the idea of a productive reason, which under certain conditions (integral to these being the 'givenness' of content) constituted its object. But this was brought about by fracting reason into various functions, each of which was not interchangeable with the other. This breaking up of man's noetic endowments set the stage for all subsequent philosophising, and it is something which is clearly reflected in the impoverished condition of much of twentieth-century philosophy. The most novel discovery of Kant's in epistemology was that of functions which are neither mechanical nor teleological, the exposition of which we find in the transcendental deduction of the categories, and it is not for nothing that Kant himself regarded this as the most important part of his *Critique*. But this, as Husserl saw, was brought about at a price, the sundering of form from matter, and the highlighting of procedural rules. Whether or not we agree with the way Kant regarded the latter as a unique kind of 'synthetic' subsumption which is set apart from the work of mere classification, the fact remains that their *rule* character was unmistakable, as also the point that they were geared to the noetic quest of fact. Now the purport of the Transcendental Dialectic was to show that the speculative ventures of pure reason may serve a useful function in enabling us to see facts in a certain light. This seeing of reason's essential work as a thrusting beyond, guided by certain key concepts, shows a much profounder insight into the metaphysical impulse than the trivial analysis in terms of picture-using provided by Wittgenstein and his devotees. What the post-Kantian idealists did was, in large part, to try to *recover* the lost unity of reason which Kant had segmented into various faculties, following the faculty psychology of his day, likewise to iron out the distinction between phenomenal and noumenal, and in so doing to refurbish both the pedigree of thought and its destiny. One of their major insights was to find in metaphysical thinking something quite disparate from the sphere of the mathematical, in other words to pinpoint its non-linear character. Their attendant assumption that there must therefore be another sort of logic at work and their finding of this in the Hegelian triadic logic is in effect a separate thesis. The non-linearity of much of philosophical thinking can be granted without accepting the Hegelian dialectical method. This is a point to which reference will be made later in the discussion.

The romantics are usually seen as standing in a relation of polarity to the thinkers of the Enlightenment. On such a showing, Kant would be classified squarely with the latter. And yet the romantics are close to Kant in perhaps their chief presupposition, that the key to the real is found in the depths of human nature rather than anywhere else. The link between the metaphysical idealists and the romantics is found in their fascination with the many dimensions of consciousness, their interest in creativity, in organic wholes, their eye for discontinuities no less than continuities, their nostalgia for the infinite. All these interests were expressed at a time when the biological sciences were coming to the fore as providers of grist for the philosophical mill. So it was not surprising that what writers wrote about at this time was often 'life' rather than 'thought'. The philosophers were, after all, up against a difficulty. Can there be a conceptual reconstruction of a dynamic process? Only if one and the same principle be at work in thought and reality. And, if this is so, philosophy must needs be systematic, otherwise it could hardly bring out the rational structure of reality.

It is at this point that metaphysical idealism and romanticism move in opposite directions, for the romantics found in system all that they disliked. Friedrich Schlegel's advocacy of a method of intuitive insight rather than deductive reasoning for philosophy was intended to assimilate philosophy to poetry. This is interesting, not only for its bringing together two spheres which almost everyone else had insisted on keeping apart, but for another reason. Schlegel shares the assumption made by many philosophers and literary critics that poetry has no conceptual element, that it involves a kind of immediate and near-magical embodiment of insights in verbal form. This is an assumption which only those who have never grappled with the writing of poetry could dare to make. Schlegel's work typifies the romantic's rejection of system. The romantic, moreover, tended to embrace contradiction rather than sublate it, to plunge into the 'schwer und dunkel' rather than to see them transmuted through the working of the *Zeitgeist* into the triumphant light of reason.

The notion of 'striving', however, has etymological affinities with that of strife, and we find as a recurrent theme in philosophers from Fichte onwards the idea of an 'other' to thought, a counter principle, in fact a rather non-Aristotelian interpretation of teleological movement. The different ways the theme appeared were, moreover, tied up with the role cast for imagination. In Fichte the productive power of imagination is none other than the activity of the absolute ego operating at an unconscious level. But, as consciousness develops, the ego rises above this level, although pure self-consciousness can only be approximated to. Reflection, whether rudimentary or not, is not, for Fichte, a purely intellectual matter. It involves feeling, moral striving, indeed man's total nature, including his instincts and impulses. The goal of all this he saw not as theoretic vision but in terms of moral consciousness. In this respect Fichte's 'ladder of ascent' is very different from Leibniz's climb from the unclear to the clear. Fichte, one could even say, is almost Humean in his refusal to rank sub-conscious drives (Trieben) as in any way lower than the more avowedly rational parts of his nature. Also he is Humean in regarding feeling as the main source of our belief in reality. Or rather he is in a key which both Hume and Rousseau share. And yet Fichte's own conception of reality is essentially ethical, and the moral order for him would be unintelligible without the divine will. But it is his interest in the total range of man's consciousness which is our concern here. It was an interest continued by Schelling.

Schelling's *System of Transcendental Idealism* discovers in aesthetic creation a unity of the unconscious and conscious mind. In common with many of his contemporaries Schelling was struck by the apparently unconscious artistry of the man of genius. To 'explain' this by inspiration, by a daemon, an infusion of divine powers, was not far from the further step which Schelling himself took, to find in the power which operates through the creative artist the same power which operates in nature, nature which for him is the "still unconscious poetry of the spirit".[12] The kinship between the poet and the philosopher is discussed by him in *Bruno* (1802) where he not only finds a metaphysical significance in works of art, but goes on to find a common concern in each with 'divine ideas'. There is, in fact, far more of romanticism in Schelling than in Fichte. Schelling goes on to work out the way in which poetry deals with myth, a field in which he was greatly interested. This can be regarded as a way of demarcating poetry and philosophy, although not altogether so, for Plato utilises myths in his own philosophical writing. However, this was not a distinction which Schelling found as compelling as the one between mythology and revelation in connection with which he gives his own interpretation of Christian theology.

Schopenhauer finds a kinship between philosophy and poetry in at least one respect: "To enrich the concept from intuition is the constant concern of poetry and philosophy." Amidst a detailed classification of the various arts he refers to the 'material' of poetry as concepts, but concepts made less abstract through the use of epithets which lend concreteness and perceptual colour to the ideas. Of the forms of poetry, tragedy is the most sublime according to Schopenhauer, in so far as it represents man's most poignant experiences. Schopenhauer is an important figure in the development of a tendency which provides a theme in the somewhat contrapuntal structure of this chapter, the tendency for the faculty of reason to be interpreted in far less 'pure' a manner in later German thought than, say, in the early rationalist philosophers like Wolff. Reason is seen as an instrument for living by Schopenhauer, and this links him in an unexpected way not only with Bergson but with the pragmatists.

Kant's critique of pure reason, after all, bore diverse and often strange fruit. It is easy to see in Schopenhauer the apostle of irrationalism, the extoller of will. From another point of view he exposes the pedigree of reason in a way

[12] *Werke*, II, p. 349.

which roots it in concrete living, an exposure which so far from downgrading it to the level of the merely manipulative, could be seen as giving it an empirical grounding the lack of which its critics had always bemoaned.

The message of the post-Kantians was different no doubt. Inter alia it included an awareness of the purposiveness of reflection, and a sense that consciousness was structured in a way which did not owe *everything* to the intellect. To the Hegelians and their successors the imagination could, above all, find fullest play in the understanding of history. But while imagination could well serve as a disinterested tool of contemplation in art, we do not view the affairs of men in as detached a manner, even though they be in the past. Imagination became the tool of philosophy à thèse, that is, of ideology, in Marx, where in apocalyptic fashion the carrot of the classless society is dangled before the eager revolutionary with an eye to changing reality. Imagination serves to inform us whence we have come and whither we may go. If anything qualifies for Kant's epithet "imaginative fiction", it is the notion of the classless society. It was a fiction reckoned to guide action instead of thought, but it interestingly enough posited a *telos* in a process which otherwise prided itself on its inevitability. It only goes to show that even a dialectic of social change which sailed under the banner of rationality could not avoid implicit reliance on the 'work' of the imagination, in the hope that this would be 'productive' in a way never anticipated by Kant.

But while records of the follies of man are necessarily shaped in some degree by psychological factors (recognition of the factors of attitude and viewpoint is quite cheerfully assimilated in present-day interest in historiography for example), the metaphysician was supposed to be above such things. For this reason naturalism, and especially psychologism, was regarded by many German philosophers in the post-Hegelian period as something into which no self-respecting philosopher should lapse. For example, Rickert found the word *Geist*, beloved of nineteenth-century German philosophy, far too psychological in connotation. Understandably those who classified philosophy among the *Geisteswissenschaften* shunned naturalism. But it was a philosopher of this kind who, paradoxically, was close to granting to the psychological foundations of world-views an importance which he thought would not be in fact as damaging to the edifice as some had feared. This was Wilhelm Dilthey.

To appreciate what he did, we need to go back to Kant once more. Kant's way of identifying a 'level' which is other than the naturalistic is through his discovery of the transcendental. The transcendental in turn is explicated through the notion of synthesis. But the whole possibility of synthesis, that is, of 'connecting' operations, presupposes an atomistic psychology where unstructured particulars, not *Gestalten*, are given. Kant's whole epistemology, in this rather surprising manner, presupposes the very psychology against which he had so firmly turned his back. To deny the original disconnectedness, to substitute *Erlebnis* for *Erfahrung*, is, ipso facto, to remove the need for synthesis. It also opened the way for seeing *Erlebnisse* as fed from diverse sources. This should not be seen as a capitulation to psychologism, but as making room for a notion of structure in terms of both depth and reach.

Dilthey was surely right to find in poetry and history modes of writing which *draw on* experience in distinctive ways. Dilthey came to the task of the analysis of the poetic and historical imagination armed with a very different conception of *Verstehen* and its functions from that of Kant. Both poetry and history fasten not on an abstracted content but on concrete particularity seen in the light of an individual perspective, that is through the lens of vision of a particular personality. We do not on this account bewail the distance the poet or the historian has put between himself and fact. Rather each throws his own idiosyncratic light on the manifold which is around us. The insights of both are confirmed in the experiential continuum which is our daily bread, and their vision lights up our own as wick enlightens wick. This is a process for which the word verification is inappropriate, but it provides a confirmation in experience of no less strength and veracity. For Dilthey, as for Husserl, articulated meanings are not to be validified by any criteria external to them. To understand them is neither to subsume them under laws, nor 'identify' them by reference to regular usage. To understand poetry and history requires an integration of imagination and reflection of the order that we already have in our own self-awareness, and the latter is in turn enriched by the work of the poet and the historian. The historian and the philosopher are alike in being in a sense at one remove from what they write about. Another way of putting this is to say that neither can resort to "having a look". Dilthey, like Lonergan in our day, is impatient with those who oversimplify the quest for knowledge. The density of things and events is not totally opaque, but neither is it so transparent as to need no labour in the articulation thereof. The Rankean desire to see "what actually happened" is analogous to the philosopher's quest for "what is". But in each case we are rather like Fritz Mauthner's clown, teetering on a ladder held by ourselves. Moreover, in all the disciplines which involve words, whether poetry, history or philosophy, the very insight is mediated through its articulation.

The stratum notion proves suggestive when we examine the idea of articulation, for it comes in in more than one context. The historical consciousness sees successive periods as stratified, the contemporary resting on the invisible layers of the past. Man's own conscious life, moreover, is stratified, consciousness itself reaching down in depth to regions which are inaccessible to introspection. The stratum idea is, of course, a metaphor. But the geological connotations of upthrust and the like contained in it provide a rather more fertile speculative tool than the idea of 'levels' with its suggestion of neat parallel regions and smooth transitions to and fro. It provides a non-linear model, appropriate in elucidating all man's cultural products which are intimately fed by his psychic life. Dilthey's classification of philosophy along with history and poetry among the *Geisteswissenschaften* is a crucial classification, for it guides us to those springs within the psyche which lead out in non-linear ways, but which nonetheless issue in *discovery*. Furthermore, his stratified way of understanding consciousness provides an alternative to the stark dichotomy between rational and irrational which has forced the greater part of philosophical treatments of thought in the western tradition into an unwearable straightjacket. Looking back, one can, admittedly, detect how much is un-Kantian about it. The form/matter distinction is left behind, likewise the demarcations of faculty psychology. There is a transgression, moreover, from a phenomenological point of view, for unlike Husserl, Dilthey does not differentiate between the transcendental and the empirical. A major reason why Dilthey does not do so is his desire to vindicate the *unity* of the person. For Dilthey, psychic life does not "constitute itself from elements; it is not a composition...it is originally and always an encompassing unity. From this unity psychic functions have differentiated themselves, but remain bound to their context. This fact, whose highest expression is unity of consciousness and the unity of the person, entirely distinguishes psychic life from the whole physical world."[13]

It is only fair to say that Husserl was no less concerned with vindicating the unity of the person and this can be illustrated from the following passage which is very evidently directed against Hume: "Consciousness is not a title-name for 'psychical complexes', for fused 'contents', for 'bundles', or streams of 'sensations', which, meaningless in themselves, could give forth no 'meaning', however compactly massed they might be; ..."[14] Husserl is concerned to stress the non-naturalist concern of the phenomenologist's programme for much the same reason that the idealists in general (and Coleridge also) rejected associationism, that is, from a conviction that the life of thought was above all else non-mechanical, and that to stress this was ipso facto to reject the view implied in the famous words "the mind and its place in nature". To speak of the *Weltlichkeit* of consciousness, or to say that man as a total person has a *Lebenswelt*, was not to lapse into naturalism. If it ruled out the philosopher's traditional quest of a vision *sub specie aeternitatis* it did something else instead, namely, it gave thought the weighty credentials of a rootedness in life. And if we must still speak of 'reason' this would be an enriched reason, not a truncated reason condemned to the measured steps of linear argument, the three-legged races of the dialectician or the monolithic implicatory judgements of the coherentist.

The difficulties need not be minimised. Dilthey made much of the distinction between the discontinuities of nature and the continuum of psychic life. He writes that in the *Naturwissenschaften*, "the continuum of nature is given only through inference, by means of the connection of hypotheses. For the

[13] *Gesammelte Schriften*, V, 211.
[14] *Ideas* (Eng. Edition) p. 251.

Geisteswissenschaften, on the other hand...a continuum of psychic life is given as primary and fundamental".[15] This is to ignore the radical discontinuities of psychic life (including not only pathological experience but the experiences of sleep, day-dreaming, lapses of attention and so on) and the fact that whatever we know of unconscious life through Freud and Jung is based on hypotheses designed to provide *explanations* of the data we have (such as dreams, slips of the tongue, neurotic phenomena etc.). But, to Dilthey, explanation and understanding are to be seen in contrast to one another, the former being appropriate to nature and the latter to psychic life. And yet the two overlap if we take seriously what he says in the *Ideen*[16]: "We explain through purely intellectual processes, but we understand through the cooperation of all our psychic powers (Gemütskräfte)...."

Dilthey's analysis of how this cooperation of psychic powers comes about is important on many counts. He saw it as a way of attacking the determinism of the associationists, as a major tool in formulating a theory of the poetic imagination, and as a key in understanding the link between poetic and historical imagination. That, in trying to describe psychic processes, we cannot help using figures of speech taken from the external world was not found, as Bergson found it to be, a radical mistake, but as inevitable, given that the *Naturwissenschaften* have shot ahead of the *Geisteswissenschaften*.[17] Our use of metaphoric language, therefore, is understandable. In exploring the metamorphosis which goes on in psychic life, Dilthey drew attention to the element of fusion, a term taken up latter by Gadamer. That the nexus (*Zusammenhang*) of psychic life was coloured by feeling and volitional activity was a point that needed making in the discussion of the poetic imagination. But if psychic life is a continuum, a matter which, as we saw earlier, he tends to overstate, in his rebound from the associationists, we would expect to find this true of its expressions outside poetry as well.

Dilthey's conception of acquired psychic nexus (erworbener seelischer Zusammenhang)[18] brought out the basic interrelatedness in an individual's experience, something concretely operative throughout his life-history. That "which is present in consciousness is oriented towards it, as well as bounded, determined and grounded by it".[19] This is a bold attempt to break through the distinction between empirical, transcendental and ontological engrained in Kant's teaching. Moreover, it represents a definitive breakaway from faculty psychology. Its importance can be regarded as far-reaching for the human studies, especially for the borderline areas between philosophy, religion and art where man goes beyond his daily octave stretch in search of new

---

[15]*Gesammelte Schriften*, V, 143-44.
[16]"Ideen über eine beschreibende und zergliedernde Psychologie".
[17]*Gesammelte Schriften*, VI, 140.
[18]*Ibid.*, VI, 90-102.
[19]*Ibid.*, VI, 143.

expressiveness. Dilthey's work carries much further the line of investigation of men like Tetens who tried to probe the nerve of *Denkkraft*, calling upon the total repertoire of human powers instead of confining concern to the Enlightenment preoccupation with "reason". Dilthey finds in imagination something which has its own structure, and which above all issues in symbolic articulation. Further, Dilthey believed that not only poetry but philosophy too, witnessed to an intensification of experience; again, something which is foreign to the *Naturwissenschaften*. The bringing together of the imaginative and the reflective can be seen more easily in poetic embodiment. But whereas the poetic task of condensation (verdichten) is in essence a making denser or more concrete, the philosophic 'condensation' is non-iconic. But its non-iconic character does not mean that imagination has no part to play in philosophic inventiveness. Philosophy, however, one could say 'suffers' in comparison to religion and poetry, in being further from an experiential dynamic base than religion or poetry.[20]

To return to Dilthey, in working out the role of creative imagination, he abandoned the organic analogies used by Coleridge and Schleiermacher, and to this extent detached himself from the romantic tradition. In its place he envisaged what he called anthropological reflection which lies "at the root where the *Erlebnis* and *Verstehen* of the poet, the artist, the religious person and the philosopher come together".[21] Such reflection, the indications are, would be concerned with meaning, with life rather than with the psyche, and involve excursions which fall neatly into neither the intuitive nor discursive basket. One does not start, Cartesian fashion, from a starting point and proceed in a linear way, but rather from a focal point, fanning outwards and plumbing depth-wise. The structured character of life itself provides a myriad of such foci. These could be contrasted with the knots or puzzles which set the linguistic practitioner on his way. One fans out from a focus neither through dialectic nor by leaning on the Jacob's staff of linguistic usage. The resonances of language can, however, *help* us in the task of anthropological reflection.

The aural implication of this must not be missed. Dilthey saw in music an art form concerned with general meaning,[22] that is to say, where the specific meanings of representationism have been left behind. In this sense, music is a perfect language. Now all pictorial images in language carry with them an echo of representationism and the image of picture-using, especially, is laden with the idea of peering at reality, albeit through a filter, taking a look and so on. Just as the full scope of the medium gets proper recognition only when the representational ideal of art is abandoned, so recognition of the 'power' of words can come only after the picture theory is abandoned. Not only the

[20] This is implied passim in Dilthey's *Das Wesen der Philosophie*, 1907.
[21] *Gesammelte Schriften*, VII, 266.
[22] *Von deutscher Dichtung und Musik*, 224.

poet, but the philosopher too, calls upon the power of *Sprachphantasie*,[23] linguistic imagination, which in turn is grounded in *Erlebnisphantasie*, or experiential imagination. The notion of metamorphosis or transformation, in Dilthey, provides the answer to those who see in all this an elaboration of naturalism. The idea of metamorphosis is well illustrated in the thematic transformations of instrumental compositions, a non-causal mode of the working out of ideas. It will also be found in philosophical prose. Linguistic imagination can be seen both as a product and as a vehicle for the expression of insight. To go further into this will take us to the role of metaphor in philosophical thinking. But the clues left by Dilthey are highly valuable ones which will guide us on our way.

---

[23] A term used in *Gesammelte Schriften*, VI, 310.

CHAPTER III

Language Games and Linguistic Imagination

It is one of the ironies of the history of philosophy that attempts to clarify the language of philosophy have in fact had a corrosive effect on the whole enterprise, especially in the case of metaphysics, calling into question the very attempts themselves. The attempts started off on the wrong foot by having models in mind which of necessity could not apply elsewhere, those of mathematics and the natural sciences. Another mistake was to look upon philosophical enquiry as one which had a natural *terminus*. Just as the terminus of the sciences was the discovery of fact so the terminus for the analyst was assumed to be the description of usage. In embarking on this programme the analyst concocted a sense of 'concept' which would have surprised the Platonist no less than the Kantian. The 'concepts', 'conceptual frameworks' and the like of the analyst are reckoned to supply a kind of gilt-edged coinage – the metaphor has overtones that are not inappropriate. What is in currency can be produced on demand, identified, underpinning the economy of everyday life and so on. Linguists, however, already know that the way we talk is far more open to change than analysts usually recognise. Anthropologists and psychologists, whose professional concern is with attitudes, beliefs, contexts and hinterlands, can ditto this. Again, the assumption that the appeals to what is 'mental' and what is 'said' are necessarily alternative strategies can be shown up as baseless if we look at the 'in' disciplines such as management studies and the clinical side of psychology. If one is to concentrate on the turbulent arena of language one willynilly must deal with the roots out of which it grows. Ah, it may be objected – this is already recognised in speaking of 'forms of life'. We have yet to see if the 'concept' of form of life can do duty for the sort of thing we have in mind. Wittgenstein very evidently is the philosopher who, since the time of Dilthey, is most self-consciously aware of the peculiarity of the philosopher's job, the almost "Pelagian", involuted nature of the language used by philosophers themselves. He also uses a number of striking figurative expressions himself, whose success or unsuccess throws up in no small part the difficulty of "speaking philosophically". It is necessary, then, to turn next to one who in many ways exerts a spell over a large number of philosophers today, oddly enough inducing a kind of cramp in them in a manner which would have dismayed Wittgenstein himself.

The matter begins, needless to say, with how we see the major change in standpoint marked by the shift from the *Tractatus* to the *Philosophical Investigations*. The *Tractatus* assumed an identity of structure between language and reality.[1] This identity was suggested through the use of a metaphor, that of picturing. Russell, at roughly the same time, and in similar vein, talked about the correspondence theory of truth. It was in a sense a 'builder's model', focusing not on the activity of building but on the bricks, the units out of which the whole was made. The link between the *Tractatus* and British realism is undisputed. What is less readily conceded by Wittgensteinians is that Wittgenstein never really gave up the guiding thread of 'taking a look' even when he shifted from the metaphor of pictures to that of tools. One reason for this may be his relative freedom from connection with academic philosophy, especially that of the German speaking tradition, a tradition whose stock in trade was judgement and discourse rather than 'looking'. The shift in his later phase can also appear as an adoption of the main lesson bequeathed by the British empiricist tradition, the decision to abandon all forms of reification. It was not a lesson which they had all managed to carry out successfully. For example, Hume's perceptions or the phenomenalists' sense data were suspiciously reified. The only lasting way to get rid of the temptation to reify was to think in terms of activities, and this is what Wittgenstein does in the *Investigations*. There is no such thing as language, there are only linguistic activities, and we are invited to 'take a look' at these.

The problem arises when we try to interpret what Wittgenstein means by game and tool. *Sprachspiel* is a single word in German. But this does not go against our seeing his use of it as analogical. The point is of some importance for the following reason. In the *Blue Book*[2] we are told that "Philosophy really *is* 'purely descriptive'." We are also told in the *Investigations*[3] that philosophy is born when language goes on holiday. It sounds as if two sorts of philosophy are being spoken of – the desirable kind, and the other kind. The holiday metaphor, incidentally is extraordinarily confusing. One does not necessarily 'idle' when on holiday. One does different sorts of things. But these are 'normal' things to be done on holidays, and indeed some of them are 'normal' things done by others on their 'working' days. For example, I may dig my garden as a recreational activity, while for a professional gardener this activity is his 'normal' way of earning a living. If one burrows beneath Wittgenstein's usage, what surfaces from time to time is a concept of the normal and the usual. We shall return to this later.

But there is a further problem. Is philosophy (of the desirable variety)

---

[1] There is a passage in the *Tractatus* where he uses 'copy' language for music, and equally unsuccessfully: "The gramophone record, the musical thought, the score, the waves of a sound, all stand to one another in that pictorial internal relation, which holds between language and the world." 4.014.
[2] P. 18.
[3] No. 38.

compatible with the use of analogies? On one view[4] there is no metaphorical intent in the term *Sprachspiel*. If we say this, we have to attribute to Wittgenstein the position that locutions actually are games, quite literally. There would also be a difficulty in pinning down which meaning of *Sprach* was most appropriate – speech, talk, locution, ways of speaking, language etc. – bearing in mind that Wittgenstein was throughout most anxious to avoid any sort of reification. But the texts do not seem to suggest this interpretation. In the *Investigations*[5] he refers to "the analogy between languages and games". This becomes clearer a little further on when he says that games are "objects of comparison which are meant to throw light on the facts of our language by way not only of similarities, but also of dissimilarities".[6] Now an analogy has a directive function and not a descriptive one, and so the more analogies are used the further one moves away from the ideal of description.

What remains is to see in what direction the analogies lead. The most important of these is surely the language game one. It was first introduced in the *Blue and Brown Books*, and in the *Investigations* about one third of the text is concerned with it one way or another. The first example, that of the builder's game,[7] appears in the context of criticising St. Augustine's Fido-Fido theory of language. The example is not a very successful one for many reasons. For example, no one would speak of building as a game (in trade union circles such a reference would have a very different 'meaning'), and if a builder called out "Block! Slab!" etc. to his assistant this would be not only an instance of getting him to do something (use) but surely of referring too. No doubt this particular example shows up the *interactive* use of language in communicative situations. It also shows another thing which for Wittgenstein was very important, that the use of words is not a total activity, that is, that the use occurs in a non-verbal context.

The similarities between conventions in a language and rules in a game are something like these. They are both customary, they function overtly, and they permit a certain amount of freedom within limitations. The last of these is especially suggestive in view of the word commonly used in German, *Spielraum*. Huizinga has analysed the various characteristics of 'play' activity, including boundedness, its 'free' character standing outside ordinary life. But what *are* the boundaries of a language game? We certainly *inherit* particular conventions and these are unlike mathematical axioms in that they are not a matter of construction or choice. But the poet does not break a convention when he says, "How like a winter hath thine absence been." Valéry has a point when he says that "the bounds of language are, on the one side, music and, on

---

[4]Max Black in conversation in Delhi in December 1978 took this line.
[5]No. 83.
[6]No. 130.
[7]This appears in *The Blue and Brown Books* (77), The *Grammatik* (PG, 57.1) and in the *Investigations* (2).

the other algebra".[8] Convention is only arbitrary bedrock if we are using literal language. But not all language games use language literally and ordinary language is full of dead metaphors.

Now Wittgenstein concedes that there can be a language game in which the purpose of words is to call up images.[9] In such cases, he says, "uttering a word is like striking a note on the keyboard of the imagination". The simile is a pianistic one and suggests the resonances which words have, although it does not bring out the interactive connotation (interaction between meaning and imagery) that figures of speech have. But if we follow this up, the 'game' resonances are not all that happy. Nor does the game analogy occur on its own but in association with the phrase 'form of life', a term which occurs only five times in his writings. This will have to be explored now.

How do we distinguish between language game and form of life in the light of the following: a language game is a language and "the actions into which it is interwoven",[10] and "Here the term 'language game' ('Sprachspiel') is meant to stress that the *speaking* of language is part of an activity, or of a form of life."[11] A further intriguing reference to 'psychic' factors further complicates matters. Psychic phenomena like hoping, wishing, regretting etc. are 'modifications' of "This complicated form of life",[12] the latter necessarily involving mastery of the use of a language. But to regard psychic phenomena as 'features' of a form of life is to speak all too loosely. Moreover, hoping itself is referred to as a language game. So that it seems clear that 'language game' is used in many senses. But the family resemblance between them all consists perhaps in this, that in no case is it possible (or meaningful) to ask for a *justification* of a particular language game. This is so because linguistic practices are founded on agreement or convention. But let us take this point up, assuming for the moment that this is the 'core' meaning.

Linguistic practices are certainly 'given' to the novice who is learning how to use them 'correctly'. But a linguistic practice is not immune from criticism or from change. Modern life is constantly throwing up new daily uses of language (I am not referring yet to the 'creative' uses of language). So to find in usage something almost analogous to the verificationist's 'stoppers' is to freeze something which is essentially fluid. Of course, there is a very general, and not particularly philosophical sense in which what people say is tied up with how they see life and reality. And yet one cannot read off the one from the other. For example, the English use of the verb 'meet' allows it a direct object ('I met him'), and American usage inserts the preposition "with"; but I would be unjustified in attributing Buberian overtones to the American style of

[8]*The Art of Poetry*, p. 72 (Eng. translation).
[9]*Philosophical Investigations*, 6.
[10]*Ibid.*, 7.
[11]*Ibid.*, 23.
[12]*Ibid.*, p. 174, Section I.

inter-personal relations. There is at least one major way in which the language game/form of life terminology carries with it an in-built point which does not go along with 'arbitrary bedrock' or 'givenness', and that is the fact that the whole raison d'être of the interactive stress in the terminology rests on the fact of communication. The only way of ruling out a locution (as, say, Wittgenstein does in ruling out private language), we are told, is by showing it has no communicable 'sense'. And yet, on the other hand, one could say that a great deal of the skilful use of language is directed to making others see what they *did not* see before.

Stressing the multiform (the *Bundheit*) character of language games and their interlocking with forms of life expresses an aperçu on Wittgenstein's part rather than a clearly worked out point of view. He is clearer about the reified conception of 'language' that he wants to reject than about the positive analysis of linguistic activities that he wishes to put in its place. There are hints of a non-linguistic subsoil out of which both linguistic and behavioural activities spring, but this was developed far more by F.H. Waismann than by Wittgenstein himself. Communication itself opens up new ways of speaking. To underplay the inventive element in ordinary communication is to betray a hankering for the 'copy' model of language and reality we had believed ourselves to have grown out of.

There is another aspect which has not been sufficiently noted – the extent to which the Viennese of Wittgenstein's generation were fond of 'word play'. It comes into Freud's psychopathology of everyday life, and Schoenberg's letters contain references to musical 'picture-puzzles'. Puzzles were, for the Viennese, not necessarily things to agonize over. Often the proper response was to enjoy them, to chuckle over them. The way in which a musical notation differs from a piece of prose has a direct bearing, I believe, on the difference between the standpoint of the *Tractatus* and the *Investigations*. But to explore this would involve saying much more about music than is proper here.

We now turn to the tool-kit metaphor which, for Wittgenstein, along with the analogy between language and games, serves to indicate the diverse functions of linguistic activity. These are Wittgenstein's major metaphors, although there are several others, which throw a lot of light on his own philosophical thinking. Incidentally there is disagreement among the commentators as to whether or not they are metaphors. Ayer speaks of metaphors,[13] Mundle of similes,[14] and Max Black of extended senses. He compares words to tools such as the hammer, pliers, saw etc. in the context of emphasising their function, their instrumental nature.[15] But language itself is also spoken of in this way: "Language is an instrument. Its concepts are instruments."[16] Both the

---

[13] In *The Concept of a Person*, in the chapter on philosophy and language.
[14] Vide *A Critique of Linguistic Philosophy*, p. 162 ff.
[15] *Philosophical Investigations*, No. 11.
[16] *Ibid.*, No. 569.

language game metaphor and the tools[17] metaphor negatively point up his departure from the picture theory, and positively highlight diversity of function. The tool-kit metaphor in fact does not serve him all that well. The engineer's tool-kit contains tools intended for specific jobs. Outside the tool-kit, however, there can be objects which we use as tools when the 'proper' tool is not at hand. There are also tools which have multiple functions (some pen-knives, for example). Moreover, we understanding the 'nature' of tools in relation to human activities which are their raison d'être. A tool is hardly 'given'; it is *made* for a particular purpose. We can sharpen a tool (for example a pencil), change it (adjust the 'bite' of a saw), discard it (after it gets broken or blunt), use a tool for a new purpose (pick a lock with an instrument other than a jemmy), and, above all, we can *improvise* tools with whatever materials be at hand. The important thing is to 'get the job done'. Some of these connotations, so far from pointing to a legislative use of language (word 'X' can function in sentence frame 'Y' like *this* and not like *that*) lead in a different direction, especially to the agent, that is to the speaker who has something he wants to say.

Both metaphors, however, throw up, in a curious way, Wittgenstein's fascination with the ideal of boundedness. It is an idea which turns up in some form or other in many of his expressions. We 'bump our heads' against the limits of language.[18] And yet the limits cannot be *shown*. The extension of a concept is "*not* closed by a frontier"[19] and we "do not know the boundaries because none have been drawn".[20] In comparing games he uses another topographical metaphor; we find "a complicated network of similarities overlapping and criss-crossing". The image is without an axis or centre, an open figure. The thread metaphor too suggests something without a core, for "the strength of the thread does not reside in the fact that some one fibre runs through its whole length, but in the overlapping of many fibres".[21] The limit idea is there again in the famous fly bottle metaphor, but it is there paradoxically, if we put it together with the 'bumping' metaphor. The person who is misguided enough to bump himself against the limits of language is actually in the fly bottle. But what would it be like to be out of the fly bottle? Presumably one would be *free*. But being free in this sense is not even to be tempted to run one's head etc. So the free man is the one who is not aware of the limits but keeps within them thanks to not being a philosopher. Language is not to go on a holiday, but to do work. Altogether it seems clear that what Wittgenstein does when he talks about beetles, flies, bumps and threads is

---

[17] Apropos my remarks a little later about serial compositions, the serial technique has been referred to as 'kit' by composers who use it.
[18] *Philosophical Investigations*, No. 119.
[19] *Ibid.*, No. 68.
[20] *Ibid.*, No. 69.
[21] *Ibid.*, No. 67.

neither to propound theses or theories, still less to describe how we actually talk. His own precept and practice with respect to the latter falls apart, but falls apart in an interesting way. The seminal points in Wittgenstein's work are not presented in *arguments* but in the form of insights expressed in figurative language. To do this is ipso facto *not* to demarcate the *Spielraum* of the expressions used. The reader is invited to see for himself where the associations lead. It is ironical indeed that a thinker whose coinage of thought was not really *concepts* at all should have fathered a generation of philosophers who have no other concern than this. To speak of language games is not to speak in an ordinary way, although the words 'language' and 'game' are ordinary words (i.e. they are neologisms). Similarly, the musical note appears in a different light in the atonal composition from what it does in the diatonic scale.

Here I have a suggestion to make. My hunch is that the distance between the *Tractatus* and the *Investigations* is advisedly analogous to the difference between tonal and atonal music. Once the moorings of tonality are gone, in a way, anything goes. And yet in a sense it is wrong to speak of atonal music as aleatory. Just *any* sequence of notes will not do; the idiosyncrasy platitude does not mean that you can say *anything* you like. But a nostalgic looking back at tonality will not help any more than a nostalgic glance at formal systems will help the philosopher. There is no alternative to striking out on one's own. One's material is still sound, is still language. But one has to listen in a different way, attuned to an inner logic, to give up the quest for correspondences, the return to the tonic. The musical thinking of Wittgenstein's own time in Vienna was on these lines, and in many ways his thinking is the philosophical counterpart of the Viennese experimentalism which was at work in all the arts, but most of all in music.

In the *Philosophical Investigations,* Wittgenstein makes this significant comment, "...It is the field of force of a word that is decisive." (230e) This could very well have been said by Schoenberg with respect to the musical note. What is the *Spielraum* of the note once it is liberated from the framework of the diatonic scale? What is the 'weight' of the word once it is lifted from the framework of correspondences? Moreover, avant-garde composers were faced with the problem of notation just as Wittgenstein was wrestling with the problem of description. Schoenberg was one of those who insisted that there was a "right" way his compositions should be performed. There was a "way to solve the musical picture-puzzles"[22] that his works constituted. But not all musical thoughts could be realised "with inexorable severity". The time would come when a worksheet would look very different from a score. The rest of the story takes us too far from our theme.

Yet the parallelism of tonality with formal systems is a very telling one.

---

[22]Schoenberg, *Letters*, p. 74, ed. Erwin Stein, trs. Eithne, Wilkins and Ernest Kaiser (New York, St. Martin's Press, Inc., 1965).

What precisely one is in for once one leaves these havens of certainty and lucidity is difficult to say. With what Schoenberg called "the emancipation of the dissonance", 'normality' ceased to be the system of 24 major and minor diatonic keys. To be free from key-relationship is like being free from the picture theory of meaning. The reaction to disintegrating key-systems parallels disillusionment with grammar (the grammar of the grammarians). Lots of sequences of sound can be made. Lots of things can be said. The atonal composition is intrinsically unbounded. There are compositions whose vocal lines can be 'assembled' in alternative ways, just as the fibres of the thread can be 'bonded' in various ways. To hold together metaphor, argument and example is a task whose difficulty is not unlike that which faces the atonal composer. What is at work cannot be described as "the thrust of the argument" in the one case, or "the theme" in the other. In both we encounter the untidy, gnomic, incomplete, and the disturbing.

But the gap between Wittgenstein's practice and precept is so great that the novelty of his own technique remains obscured. His relation to empiricism is more like that of Hegel to Kant, for he refuses to take over the empiricist's simplistic demarcation between sense and nonsense as Hegel refused to accept the stark either/or of the Kantian Antinomies. If philosophy be regarded as a game where one makes the rules as one goes along (as one does in an atonal composition) it is obviously not the sort of game where one can be said to 'win'. It is more like a performance which others watch with interest, as one watches something experimental and intriguing in the performative arts. And naturally questions of truth and falsity will not arise. The philosopher then, par excellence, is the inventor of a new language game. But, if this be granted, there is no way of *ruling out* a game that may not be to our liking. Moreover, the big *disadvantage* in regarding philosophy in this way is that it leaves out the consideration that language is only of interest if the person using it has in fact *something to say*. And having something to say cannot be divorced from the non-linguistic subsoil out of which linguistic expression grows. Wittgenstein's linguistic imagination enables him to coin a number of catchy phrases. His very difficulty in reconciling these with each other brings out the crucial task the philosopher, any philosopher, has in employing metaphor, argument and example.

There is one other way in which Wittgenstein's position can be put if my earlier references to music are taken into account. His lurking retention of the idea of 'normal' usage is rather like the backward and longing look an atonal composer may have in the direction of tonality. To carry out in a thoroughgoing way the full implications of the language game concept is to *abandon* the goal of description, just as to abandon tonality involves leaving behind once and for all the idea of "resolution". But this last step Wittgenstein was not able to take. It involved leaving the bounded figures of the designer's drawing board for the explosive canvases of Kandinsky. But it is with Kandinsky, Calder,

Gertrude Stein and John Cage that he, in the last analysis, belongs.[23]

Waismann's work, in my view, takes us a stage further in exploring the nerve of what I call linguistic imagination. In his *How I See Philosophy* he uses a very suggestive kind of prose to put across his ideas. The philosopher is said to be "a man who senses as it were hidden crevices in the build of our concepts where others see the smooth path of commonplaceness before them".[24] Our different expressions show we are "using different pictures, each in its way quite appropriate to the occasion"; yet when we try "to apply them jointly they clash".[25] He takes the example of time. If we say "time flows *through* the 'now' " it suggests that time is moving while the onlooker is still. But to say that "the moment flies" suggests that the onlooker is moving through time. It is "precisely because of its elusiveness that time catches our imagination". The whole passage deserves quoting: "As we all know what time is, and yet cannot say what it is, it feels mystifying; and precisely because of its elusiveness it catches our imagination. The more we look at it we are puzzled: it seems charged with paradoxes."[26] He diagnoses the mystifying factor in the noun form "the time". What we do when we worry away at such problems is to try "to catch the shadows cast by the opacities of speech".[27] All this raises many questions. Of the two sentences about time, the first is surely a philosopher's sentence, and the second is not. In what sense is time elusive? We seem to "know what time is" and yet cannot *say* what it is. But are our locutions about time opaque, or are they peculiarly suggestive and appropriate? Does language not perhaps come to our assistance when we formulate the following:

Time like an ever rolling stream
Bears all its sons away

On another occasion it may be appropriate to say "Time stood still." We do not, in fact, apply these expressions jointly, and only a philosopher would think of doing so. Is to speak of "days and moments quickly flying" to speak opaquely or to speak transparently? Some may take the latter view. He advises, "A wrong analogy absorbed in the forms of our language produces mental discomfort."[28] But how are we to distinguish between wrong analogies and right analogies? There have been many commentators who believe that Wittgenstein's use of the word 'game' in connection with language is infelicitous, and some have listed the ways in which languages/locutions etc.

---

[23]Cf. F. Waismann's remark in the last decade of his life that the "one important quality" of a philosophy is "to give expression to the major trends of the time", *Philosophical Papers*, Ed. by Brian McGuinness, Reidel, 1977, p. 146.
[24]Published by Macmillan, 1968, p. 2.
[25]*Ibid.*, p. 5.
[26]*Ibid.*, p. 5.
[27]*Ibid.*, p. 6.
[28]*Ibid.*, p. 6.

are not like games at all. There are others who point out positive ways in which languages do resemble games. Should we see which side wins, or rather hunt out the core meaning which Wittgenstein wanted to get across? Shall we not say that analogies can be good or bad rather than right or wrong? Analogies do not add to opacity; they rather break it up, creating, so to say, apertures through which light can fall. This is so no less with the analogies philosophers may use than with the figurative expressions of everyday speech.

The analogies we use are linked to the very "subsoil of language"[29] and it was one of Waismann's most important contributions that he drew our attention to this. Any current experience is embedded in a "vast background" and language adapts itself to this. So there is an "unmeasured sum of experience stored up in the use of our words and syntactical forms".[30] Now if experience is "stored" in language this explains why words move us and why the very nerve of argument is "informed" with the resonance of past experience. The unmeasured sum of experience is the non-linguistic subsoil which nourishes language. If this is so, so far from speaking of the opacity of linguistic expressions, we need rather to be sensitive to the nuanced character that they have. The subsoil idea directs us not to a 'reality' conceived in external terms, but to a matrix out of which language has a natural birth, a matrix not restricted to the individual's experience but intimately related to the total heritage to which we are heir. It is the resources of this heritage which provide not only the ground and presupposition of all shared communication, but afford its very nutriment. 'Opacity' is, then, an inappropriate epithet for the expressions which set philosophical thinking in motion. Nor are we merely set on an etymological track.

If words themselves encapsulate experience, the barrier which some set up between language and reality is indeed an artificial one. Articulation comes naturally to man, not of course that all his modes of articulation speak with a single voice. The important thing is that the ramifications which help all expression on its way involve not only connections between *words*, but strata of experience from which they are in no way divorced. If this be so, then argument itself will be shaped and sustained thereby. We, in that case, will not see in argument a tool for dispelling "wrong analogies" (as Waismann puts it) but a peculiarly linear way of proceeding from one expression to another.

To allow philosophical discourse to remain at a merely verbal level is therefore to cut it off from its natural sources of illumination, a territory where language and reality are wedded together. The philosophical questions which dissolve (those of a purely logical or linguistic nature) and those which become assimilated in science are not of this order. But those which give birth to metaphysics are. It is necessary to note that the very marriage of language and

---

[29]*Ibid.*, p. 14.
[30]*Ibid.*, p. 14.

experience which issues in metaphysics also issues in poetry. These siblings are, however, distinct, and this fact must occupy us later.

A further consequence of recognising what Waismann calls "the vast background in which any current experience is embedded" is that the cure for cramps or mystification cannot merely be an appeal to current usage. Living thought is not necessarily unclear, but it *can* be so. The metaphor of loosening cramped positions suggests a free-wheeling use of language. Another figure from magnetic fields also suggests we need to free ourselves from "the domination of linguistic forms". Waismann speaks of the various inarticulate analogies which "act upon us, one might say, like a field of force, a language field, that draws our mental gaze in a certain direction".[31] To avoid this sense of determination we are invited to see a philosophic question "against a different linguistic background".[32] At this point one can see a trace of the Gestalt point of view familar in German-speaking intellectual circles in the thirties in the prevailing battle against associationism.

We need to return now to Waismann's view of the nature of philosophic argument. We have already noticed that he thinks that argument can dispel wrong analogies, and ourselves been critical of the concept of 'wrong analogy'. Another thing that argument can do, Waismann says, is to stress similarities with other cases and bring about a shift of perspective. This kind of task amounts to a "quiet and patient undermining of categories".[33] This in turn is supposed to lead to a "wider standpoint unobstructed by misunderstandings". He, however, distinguishes the philosophical procedure from the logical one, for philosophical arguments are not logically compelling. His point is that there is a decisional element in philosophising, whether or not we are, say, to take this case as analogous to that. In logic we are constrained "while philosophy leaves us free".[34] But philosophical argument can have force because it enables us to see things in a new way.

That Waismann recognises the limits of logic is seen in the following passage, "...a philosopher may see an important truth and yet be unable to demonstrate it by formal proof. But the fact that his arguments are not logical does nothing to detract from their rationality." He goes on to say that examples come to the rescue, for these can lead to "a new way of seeing". I have elsewhere had critical things to say about the use of examples,[35] considered why Kant eschewed them, and suggested that although an example seems to bear a resemblance to a 'crucial case' in science the resemblance is after all a spurious one. But here Waismann's focus is not only on examples per se and

---

[31]*Ibid.*, p. 19.
[32]*Ibid.*, p. 20.
[33]*Ibid.*, p. 21.
[34]*Ibid.*, p. 21.
[35]"Two views of inductive philosophizing", *Kant-Studien*, Heft 3, 1967.

the importance of what he says has in my view been missed by those whose attention is centred on Wittgenstein.

A philosophical procedure may include an argument but it may not entirely *consist* in argument. This seems to be what Waismann invites us to consider. Whether or not *arguments* are used, philosophical advance is made when we are able to see things we had not seen before. But there can be no *recipe* for opting between an old and a new categorial framework. What governs our decision that a new answer fits a philosophical question? And does a question disappear when a new answer is given to it? A new, "good" answer may dissolve a question, or it may allow the question to ramify. This is granted by Waismann. There can be no *criteria* for opting for a particular new perspective. Similarly, there can be no criteria for distinguishing between linguistic forms from whose dominance "living thought" needs to escape, and the fresh "linguistic background" which will enable us to say, "Yes, that's it."

We are faced, then, both with the incrustations of language (or even the straightjacket which it can make for us) and its undoubted plasticity (a word which Waismann uses). The key to which is which, is presumably the sense of 'cramp' we may or may not have, the bewilderment which is symptomatic of muddles. The persuasive character of the philosophical enterprise is drawn attention to by Waismann. We may not, however, be persuaded that certain categories have been actually undermined (for example we may refuse to be seduced by identity-thesis theorists about the mind/body problem); or we may seek to break away from categorial thinking. To be left free ("philosophy leaves us free") is also to be free to resist persuasion. The plasticity of language is such that it yields "to the will to express, even at the price of some obscurity".[36] Philosophical issues, that is to say, are not mere skirmishes about language. The philosopher, no less than any other writer, *strives to express something*. And to have something to say is both to express an insight, and, in the very formulation thereof to sharpen and extend insight. If there is any 'circularity' about philosophical articulation it is surely this. Without something to say the philosopher remains silent. When he articulates, he both *has* something to say and is *seeking* something to say. It is in this sense that language for the philosopher becomes a tool. But for language to be merely a tool amounts to its being cut off from its original *point de départ*, the *striving* to express something which sets the philosopher on his way. Clarity can darken by nipping living thought in the bud. (Vide Waismann, *Ibid.* p. 16, "It is all very well to talk of clarity, but when it becomes an obsession it is liable to nip the living thought in the bud....For my part I've always suspected that clarity is the last refuge of those who have nothing to say.") This is not, I think, a mere facon de parler. What is hidden in the bud is not obscure. But it *is* hidden. It only comes into view when matured, when the time is ripe.

[36]*Ibid.*, p. 23.

Thinking operates at a level which is not all in the clear light of day. Our intimations are nurtured unconsciously; the extent of light increases, as in a city, with the illumination that comes from a myriad small sources. Or, to change the metaphor, we often close in on a problem, working at it from many directions. But what of obscurity? To give language its free play, to find, in the very plasticity that language has, a fitting medium for expression, is to invite an obscurity called into being by the very plenitude of what we invoke. Is this not to be contrasted with what Waismann calls "the shadows cast by the opacities of speech".[37] One must surely grant that these two senses of the obscure are different. That we need to allow language a certain free play is further conveyed by another figurative expression used by Waismann. A philosophy, he says, is "an attempt to unfreeze habits of thinking, to replace them by less stiff and restricting ones".[38]

But are these habits of thinking not precisely what we find in ordinary everyday uses of language? If so, ordinary usage no longer has any oracular power; the philosopher cannot test his own uses of language against any kind of gauge. He has to navigate, using his own judgement, faithful to his own insights, and his use of language will be neither more nor less 'normal' than that of anyone else. In a striking passage Waismann says, "... it cannot even be proved that a given expression is natural, a metaphor fitting, a question proper (or unaskable), a collocation of words expressive (or devoid of meaning). Nothing of the sort can be demonstrated."[39] The question whether an expression can be said to be natural or not will arise later on when we examine the notion of metaphor.

But what is truth? Is the philosopher at all concerned with it? Waismann here shows an ambivalence, which is interesting in view of the general linguistic analytic stance that a philosopher's statements are neither true nor false. On the one hand he says that "... a philosopher may see an important truth and yet be unable to demonstrate it by formal proof".[40] And yet a little later he makes a distinction between "the scientist's aim to find new truths and the philosopher's aim to gain insight".[41] Admittedly, this insight does not follow from deducing theorems from premises nor from the investigation of data in laboratory conditions. But "to see things in a new way" (p. 21) is not merely to see how words are used, and, in any case, words are used in situations and in virtue of what is believed to be the case. There is no doubt at least one case where philosophical thinking may be said to issue in something other than truth, namely when in the discussion we simply succeed in *raising questions*. And this is, on all counts, an extremely important part of philosophical

[37] *How I See Philosophy*, p. 6.
[38] *Ibid.*, p. 34.
[39] *Ibid.*, p. 24.
[40] *Ibid.*, p. 31.
[41] *Ibid.*, p. 34.

thinking. But to raise a question usually leads on to the consideration of putative answers. And this in turn raises a further set of question as to their satisfactoriness. Now at what stage, or stages, does the question of insight come in? The raising of a question can itself, surely, be evidence of insight. The finding of a 'satisfactory' answer can also be said to evince insight. But I suspect it is important not to look upon insight as a kind of 'stopper' akin to the termini of verificatory processes. An insight for the philosopher is more akin to a caravan halt than to arrival at a destination.

But would such a way of putting it put paid to any reference to truth? Can there not be "truth in so far as we are able to see it"? And does the philosopher's coinage of words and sentences make what he says any more tentative than the scientist's quantitative formulations, hedged in with qualifications as these are? Is it the open texture of language (as against the closed texture of numbers) that obliges us to hold back from any claim to truth? Cannot Waismann's own major discovery of the concept of *Porosität* be said to express a truth? We need next then to turn to open texture and see what bearing this has on what the philosopher strives to express.

Kneale's translation of *Porosität* as 'open texture' was perhaps influenced by the usual canon for 'good' translation, not to use a word with the identical root. But the overtones of 'porosity' and 'open texture' are not quite the same. Open texture suggests the loosely woven, even the diaphanous. No doubt Waismann does speak of texture, and texture is something to which more than one of the senses reacts. A porous object like chalk is capable of absorption of elements from outside, e.g. ink blots and liquids in general. In a sponge the 'gappiness' which accommodates liquid is even more. But in both cases the 'gappiness' is what makes the substance able to 'mop up' elements from outside. The gappiness recalls the crevices[42] which Waismann referred to earlier. Here is the passage. He is speaking of the philosopher as "a man who senses as it were hidden crevices in the build of our concepts where others only see the smooth path of commonplaceness before them".[43] We are here set to work thinking about the difference between the bounded and the open, the loose and the free, the frozen and the unfrozen. Now the original speaks of "Porosität der Begriffe" and 'Begriffe' are *concepts*, that is, what are classically or traditionally thought of as bounded. Think of the Socratean injunction to Glaucon to polish our concepts. The image is sculptural. The polishing is the final stage. Rough edges have already been smoothed out. What remains is the patina, the gloss. Even stone can have varying degrees of porosity. Granite, marble and sandstone are not all the same in this respect. Now a porous object can swell up if it absorbs liquid, that is, its contours can change. Waismann had in mind empirical concepts, and in particular the reason *why* the

---

[42]Loose-jointedness is intrinsic to a pluralistic universe, William James pointed out. A block universe with no cracks, could only be described by a 'blocky' term – i.e. the Absolute.
[43]*How I See Philosophy*, p. 2.

phenomenalist's programme of translatability (material object sentences into sense datum sentences) was unworkable. The crevice idea comes in again here. We cannot delimit our concepts in all possible directions. We cannot *define* so that "every nook and cranny is blocked against entry of doubt". But not that *Porosität* means vagueness, for a vague word is one which is used in a fluctuating way. This can be dealt with by making stricter rules for usage. But this remedy is not available to us in the case of concepts which are porous. When a concept is non-exhaustive, it stretches "into an open horizon". Here Waismann uses a term which Locke, Kant and Husserl had already made use of. It suggests even more a never-to-be-reached idea than does the asymptote. But Waismann advisedly avoids bringing in here mathematical analogies like the asymptote or even the 'open' figures of geometry, as all of these are tied up one way or another with rules. But he does tie in essential incompleteness with the possibility of doubt.

Even so the 'Porosität' figure of speech is highly important in analytical literature, it seems to me, because it does not suggest at all *that anything is wrong*. Waismann's metaphors in discussing all this are derived from the science of geology. What is it like when we look at a cliff face? The strata do not go in parallel lines. There can be an upthrust of a lower layer visible in a higher layer. Any particular layer, moreover, may not show a uniform density; stones, gravel, pockets etc. may be visible. A 'fault' or fracture line, enables us to peer down from above, (or even look from below) and detect some, although not all of the points, at which the strata diverge. The 'picture' recalls the model used by another fellow-Viennese – Sigmund Freud. There is a similar contrast of the seen and unseen, indeed an interplay between them, a sense of a work of detection involved in pin-pointing focal points rather than plotting causal lines.

But we must not lose sight of the *use* that Waismann makes of the metaphors. Statements in one distinct language stratum are "linked by clearly apprehended logical relations". But when we move from one stratum to another, he says, "the connection is no longer coercive – owing to the incompleteness of all our data".[44] Now is the lack of coerciveness of the chains of inference that lead from statements of one stratum to those of another due to incompleteness of the data or to the fact that we have moved to a different stratum? Waismann stresses the former, the incompleteness. No less crucial is perhaps the point that between statements belonging to two different strata "there exist no relations of the sort supplied to us by classical logic". It is not easy to unpack the meaning of the following: "The fracture lines of the strata of language are marked by philosophical problems; the problem of perception, of verification, of induction, the problem of the relation between mind and body, and so on."[45] When a fracture occurs (geologically speaking) we see the

[44]*Ibid.*, p. 50.
[45]*Ibid.*, p. 50.

strata more clearly. The strata do not collide. He is here referring to the line which marks the transition from one stratum to another. Here one may be on to something interesting, for the order of 'dependency' of the lower strata on the higher and vice versa are not the same. But just as Wittgenstein finally emancipates the game idea from rule, so Waismann emancipates the stratum idea from lower and higher. He is concerned most of all with the line of transition between one stratum and another, where "strata make contact, so to speak".[46]

Open texture, we might hazard, may lead not only to loose inferences, but to non-inferential trains of thinking. This interpretation is encouraged if we bring in at this point his frequent references to the Gestalt analyses of perception. When we see a new aspect in an ambiguous figure this is something we arrive at non-inferentially. When we see character in a face, we are not "inferring". This was said, incidentally, by Berkeley centuries ago. To recognise in a new style of painting a new way of seeing is to be convinced through other means than that of argument. We seem to be at large in a field where neither the coerciveness of linear inference nor of associative patterns of a psychological kind are the order of the day. If the main function of language is to categorise, this puts us in a bit of a spot over the language used by the philosopher. The philosopher, qua philosopher, moves about on different levels; he commutes between different language strata. In so doing he uses words which have a "systematic ambiguity". This is altogether more hopeful a situation than being condemned to the systematically misleading. The systematic ambiguity arises from moving beyond the sphere where rules are operative. Waismann's originality no doubt lies in seeing this as operative even in empirical discourse which the empiricists (especially the reductionist brand of phenomenalists) had thought to be complete, a description of knock-down evidence.

But there is another consideration too. The concept of ambiguity provides a suggestive comparison with that of antinomy, an alternative, that is to say, to the Kantian diagnosis of what happens when one goes beyond rules. Both Kant and Waismann see in philosophic thought an exploring beyond limits, an adventure into territory where there can be no definitions. Kant finds a synthetic a priori element at work within induction, and Waismann finds an open texture in empirical concepts. The shift from antinomy to ambiguity is most significant. Waismann's insight takes him beyond dichotomy to plural possibilities. The question is no longer about what can or cannot be proved, but concerns the very content of what we affirm or what we *mean* when we use a particular form of words. The onus is on the philosopher, to show us what he means, to lead us to the point where we can see as he sees. And this involves a linguistic skill, a linguistic imagination, for which no rules can be specified. Waismann at times reiterates a more conventional view, speaking of language

---

[46]*Ibid.*, p. 100.

as "a means of comprehending and categorizing differently".[47] But alongside this there is a rather more exciting admission, that among the regulative principles which guide our constructions can be included "a mere tone of thought which, though not explicitly stated, permeates the air of a historical period and inspires its leading figures. It is a sort of field organising and directing the ideas of an age".[48]

There is also the factor of style of expression. "If you ever try to put some rare and subtle experience, or a half forgotten impression, into words, you'll find that truth is intrinsically tied up with the style of your expression."[49] Now what kind of nexus do we find when matters of period and style determine the very substance of what we say? From what Waismann tells us it seems that in such cases we are not dealing with what belongs to a single stratum but to the relations between strata, and that these are of "a most complicated, peculiar and elusive nature", something more, and to which logic cannot be applied. Whether or not this should occasion dismay we have yet to see.

We are then in search of a nexus other than the deductive one, a clue to how to move from one statement to another, how to jump and which way to jump. In the course of exploring language strata Waismann reveals himself as extraordinarily sensitive to the resonances of words. He writes, "We seem at times to glimpse behind a word another sense, deeper and half hidden" and "hear faintly the entry of another meaning, in and with which others begin to sound, and all accompany the original meaning of the word like the sympathetic chimes of a bell."[50] This time Waismann speaks in tune with Herder rather than with Kant. He continues, "...the meanings interpenetrate, and unite into a larger whole, a sort of cloud...We may say that they dissolve into vagueness."[51] Waismann's images are those of reverberation of sounds (not including discords) which are in tune with each other, or visually, that of a penumbra about a network rather than about a centre. Once we have left definitions behind we have also left behind cores and centres. Kant had spoken of the metaphysician's flapping of wings in empty space. Valéry looks at wings differently. To isolate a word from its functions is to "clip its wings and it turns and rends you".

To say that the "idea of truth varies with the kind of statement"[52] was to throw down the gauntlet to the verificationists in the mid-forties of this century. It is still startling for the analyst to hear that there is nothing particularly oracular about stock uses. In analytic philosophy, there have been few to listen to Waismann's advice that "a departure from the beaten track...may be the

---

[47]*Ibid.*, p. 63.
[48]*Ibid.*, p. 63.
[49]*Ibid.*, p. 98.
[50]*Ibid.*, p. 104.
[51]*Ibid.*, p. 105.
[52]*Ibid.*, p. 112.

very thing to be striven for – in poetry, science, and in philosophy". The implications of what Waismann said have been largely lost on those who work in the analytic manner. If words are as many-textured as Waismann says (and what literary artist would ever disagree), it may be the height of 'unwisdom' to "fight against the fascination which forms of expression exert upon us".[53] We are not called upon to choose between seeing philosophical problems as concerned either with facts of the world *or* matters of expression. Philosophical writings express insights, integral to which is the manner in which they are expressed and which very much concern the way in which the world is conceived to be.

In freeing the philosopher from Wittgenstein's spurious dichotomy, Waismann yet posed him with a task of peculiar difficulty – how to know when to swim with the stream of language and when to swim against it. The skilled swimmer *knows*. And so does the philosopher. There can be no theoretical answer as to how the task is to be done. There is no occasion for being alarmed by the prospect of rapids ahead. The philosopher shares the problem that faces all writers, himself being no exception. There can be no recipe for employing the linguistic imagination. That there is such a power as the linguistic imagination the matters with which we have been concerned in this chapter leave us in no doubt. Waismann's own writings provide rich evidence of it. If it is natural to the philosopher to commute between different language strata, to explore the diverse textures of words, we are on the track of something which is no mere techné, an enterprise in which language, thinking and reality are intimately involved, and with no less intensity than for those engaged in the craft of literature.

---

[53]*The Blue Book*, p. 27.

CHAPTER IV

Metaphor and Meaning

In the preceding chapter the discussion of phrases like language games, tool-kit, and language strata suggested that these stemmed from what could be called linguistic imagination, the power of using language inventively in order to communicate meaning. The writers who have used these expressions very evidently thought that what they wished to convey could be best conveyed in this way. We may take it that they were not being deliberately obscure or using a roundabout method which could have been substituted by something more direct. We also saw that there was a certain lack of consensus as to whether these expressions should be called metaphors. At least there was lack of consensus in the case of the expression 'language game'. About some of the other expressions, e.g. bumping one's head, language going on holiday, language strata etc., there seems to be no great objection to saying that these are used metaphorically by the writers concerned. Secondly, linguistic imagination seems to be fed from a subsoil which is partly linguistic and partly non-linguistic. If, as it seems reasonable to suppose, this is connected with 'having something to say', we do not need to shy off this question in the desire to avoid naturalism. This matter will be attended to later when we consider subversion and intention, and discuss, inter alia, the contribution of Lazerowitz in this regard.

The third finding identified the peculiar difficulty that the philosopher has in the connecting of argument, metaphor and example. In all but the most stringent cases of linear argument, philosophical discourse has a certain looseness of texture which makes it very different from narrative and from the symbolic transformations of pure logic. The philosopher constantly strives to bridge gaps, to lead us to the point where we see. He makes out a case, his brief is prepared skilfully. But because of, especially, the extreme generality of what he says – and this is true of writers in the empiricist and neo-empiricist (analytic) camp no less than of the classical system builders – it is not to be taken *literally*. We have to gauge what he wants to say. Not that this should involve us in a near Sherlock Holmesian work of detection. While the generalities of the philosopher, especially of the speculative metaphysician, have given the impression of departing from literal expression, this, in turn, has been taken by some, perhaps mistakenly, to involve a departure from fact. On the other hand, the philosopher seems to have something in common with others who use metaphorical expressions, whether in everyday speech or in the craft of poetry. It is relevant, therefore, in our examination of the prose the philosopher uses, to see how metaphor and meaning are related.

We owe to Aristotle, perhaps more than to anyone else, the insight that thought *moves*. This itself is not to be taken literally. But for thinking to *dwell*, by contrast, can be seen as something intrinsically difficult. This is why in all traditions which set store on the value of contemplation the endeavour is seen as one for which great preparation is needed. The mind cannot be steadied, so to say, on a particular object, except through training, that is, through the use of certain techniques. The volatility of thought undergoes a different kind of discipline in the study of mathematics where movement is broken down into a series of ordered steps. The movement which takes place in metaphorical thinking is so different from this that it is not surprising that the mathematical mind, such as Frege's was, is often hostile to it. This is what Frege says about metaphor: "The metaphorical aspect of language presents difficulties. The sensible breaks in and makes expression metaphorical and so improper."[1] While Locke and Kant were no doubt right in fixing on the perceiving of relations as the central work of thought, neither of them discovered in metaphorical thinking a mode of relational thought which issues in discourse and which needs analysis on its own account. Locke could have arrived at this as he was 'a man of letters', exceptionally sensitive to the different kinds of thinking involved in the disparate fields of science, history, theology etc. When Kant saw fit to bifurcate *intellectus* into *Verstand* and *Vernunft*, he could yet have taken the differentiation further. The twentieth-century shift from the analysis of thinking to that of saying, unfortunate though it is in some respects (especially, as has been suggested earlier in this study, in its tendency to replace the 'mental' by the 'said'), at least has the merit of bringing into focus different *kinds* of discourse.

There is good warrant, I believe, for the current interest in metaphor on the part of some philosophers, it being no occasion for surprise that the matter has concerned literary critics ever since the time of Aristotle. The study of the logic of language in the twentieth century has been in great part taken up with the analysis of reference. On the one hand there is the work of the logicians who are concerned with sense and reference. But there are others who have drawn our attention to different kinds of *indirect* language. Freud is something of a father figure in this respect. Myths, dreams and various symbolic ways of speaking, gesturing and acting, are all found to have a meaning which is expressed indirectly. This cuts across any simple identification of the direct and the indirect with the public and the private, still less with the referent and the emotive. Psycho-analytic practice shows that it is possible to speak indirectly

---

[1] Gottlob Frege, "The Thought: a logical inquiry", *Mind*, July 1956, p. 298, footnote.

and yet highly meaningfully. It also shows that meanings sometimes have to be hunted for i.e. the simple referent is no longer the paradigm of the meaningful.

The phenomenology of language reveals that much of our speaking and writing 'points to' and that the word 'refer' is a misnomer for this kind of activity – the cultivated and subtle uses of language 'lead' and 'suggest'. They are persuasive in a manner which matches many-hued expression by many-hued understanding-responses. The metaphor in a way typifies the directive role that language has, and no one interested in the phenomenological approach to language can afford to neglect it.

The analytic philosopher, whether or not he realises it, needs to examine metaphor for the following reason. The idiosyncrasy platitude, and the linguistic polymorphism which it implies, seems to go along with what could be called a theory of 'natural kinds' with respect to linguistic usage. That this is the implication seems to be a part and parcel of the stress on *different* language games, on separate discourses. But *are* language games radically heterogeneous? Kant made a significant discovery (whose importance it is no doubt fashionable to deny these days) when in treating of mathematics he recognised that there were *both* analytic sequences and synthetic operations to be found in mathematical thinking. A great deal of post-Wittgensteinian work in ethics has pointed up the mixed character of ethical discourse. These 'mixes' are not collisions, but something integral to the texture of the thinking involved. Now to put metaphors under the microscope of analysis reveals what happens when ideas/thoughts/concepts which seem to belong to different contexts/worlds are juxtaposed, and more than juxtaposed. They, therefore, pose a challenge to all categorial thinking, to all attempts to confine thinking to the bounded, to the conceptual, in short, they pose a challenge to the impulse to *classify*.

As metaphors not only illustrate what we have called linguistic imagination, but *concrete* imagination, they highlight a meeting of the sensible and the intelligible in a way which is very pertinent to the whole metaphysical endeavour. This needs elucidation. Both metaphor and metaphysics lead us beyond. But the lesson of metaphor for the metaphysician lies in this, that the very cue for thought lies in what is *sensible*. Analogical thinking is a kind of inference. Like metaphorical thinking it begins in the perception of similitude, something for which, as Aristotle stressed, there can be no recipe. But while analogy belongs to the structure of *argument*, metaphor per se *need* not. It will later be a part of our task to show that the use of metaphor *can* be integral to argument. Admittedly more has been written on poetic metaphor than on the use of metaphor in everyday speech or in philosophic prose. This should not prevent our seeing that the link that metaphor has with the world of the senses affords it an empirical anchorage and at the same time a means of moving from the empirical to the trans-empirical. In other words, it seems to provide a mode of entry into the transcendent which could be the envy of the speculative metaphysician were it not that the latter utilises the same technique himself. But is metaphor merely a technique? The question can be raised, but not answered yet.

It is a matter of common knowledge that the influence of mathematics on philosophy has been so strong that clearness and distinctness has been a paradigm for philosophers in a considerable part of the western tradition. The paradigm found a natural place within rationalism, but it was by no means confined to it. Mainstream empiricism right up to the most recent analytic philosophy has been fascinated by clarity. Yet rationalism itself accommodated another approach, represented by Leibniz and Hegel, where clarity was by no means regarded as the prime target of thought. For both of these, however, recognition of the presence of the unclear and the indistinct was combined with a faith in the capacity of rational thought to ascend to the pure concept. Within empiricism, Berkeley is significant in his recognition of the need to *nuance* philosophical vocabulary in keeping with the distinctive features of experience. It was this consideration that led him to use the word 'notion' in a way it had not been used before. My point is that once mathematical symbols are left behind as a paradigm of clarity we are left free to utilise the whole range of language with all its capacity for nuanced expression. The current fashion for 'symbolising' in a manner as close to calculi as possible appears in a curious light. The language of abstract non-linguistic symbols is par excellence non-referential. The retreat to this language, therefore, represents a refusal "to say anything", for all the things "about which something can be said" are not susceptible to the language of calculi. Now one of the most familiar way of nuancing linguistic expression is through metaphor. So in all these various ways the examination of metaphor emerges as crucial for the philosopher who is striving to express something which cannot be *referred* to in any simplistic manner. What is *worth* saying cannot always be said clearly. The nuanced is neither the vague nor the obscure. It has to be understood on its own terms. How does one do this?

In the tradition of rhetoric, metaphor did not convey information but was confined to the role of stylistic ornament. Aristotle connected metaphors to nouns or words rather than to discourse. Metaphor was one of the figures of speech called tropes on account of the way they stemmed from a deviating use of the meaning of words. On such a view when a writer uses a metaphor he substitutes one name by another. The usual or proper word is replaced by another. The feature which governed the choice of the new word was resemblance. There is nothing trivial about metaphors in Aristotle's view, for to be a master of metaphors is "a sign of genius, since a good metaphor implies an intuitive perception of the similarity in dissimilars".[2] Moreover, "...it is from metaphor that we can best get hold of something fresh".[3] Paul Ricoeur has

---

[2] *Poetics*, 1459 a 5-8, Ingram Bywater, trans. in the Basic Works of Aristotle.
[3] *Rhetoric*, 1410 b 10-15.

pointed out[4] in criticism of the substitution theory that it cannot account for the difference between a 'bad' metaphor and a 'novel' metaphor. Nor can the theory explain the process by which the meaning of a word is extended beyond its common use. An analysis of metaphor confined to words as units could not be expected to disclose how metaphor is generated. For this we need to turn to sentences and to discourse as such.

Taking the sentence as the unit, I.A. Richards found in the metaphorical sentence a tension between what he called a tenor and a vehicle. The underlying idea is called the 'tenor' and the idea under whose sign the first idea is apprehended is the 'vehicle'. The metaphorical sentence gives us two ideas at once which interact with each other. On Richards' view a metaphorical sentence does not bring about 'fusion' of the two. The interplay between the two meanings is integral to metaphor. But what are the two? Are they thoughts, things, or ideas? And how does the insight brought about by the interaction come about? Max Black's earlier contribution on metaphor[5] brings in what he calls the "system of associated commonplaces" which is invoked by using an expression metaphorically. This enables us to explain cases where the use of the metaphor plays upon a stock of knowledge commonly held. But in the use of a *novel* metaphor something different takes place. A writer can appeal to a new system of implications and invite us to look at things in a new way. But interaction no doubt works both ways. Black puts this in his characteristically humorous way: "If to call a man a wolf is to put him in a special light, we must not forget that the metaphor makes the wolf seem more human than he otherwise would."[6] Associated commonplaces are of course not culture-free, but then neither is language. The associated implications (in Black's phrase) *may* consist of "deviant implications" established ad hoc by the writer. He further says that "the metaphor selects, emphasizes, suppresses and organises features of the principal subject by implying statements about it that normally apply to the subsidiary subject."[7]

There seems to me to be two interesting instances of lack of boundedness involved here, the connotation of what "normally" applies to the subsidiary subject, and what I would like to call the '*Spielraum*' of the metaphor. The use of *Spielraum* conveys the 'play' between the principal subject and the subsidiary one and underlines its interactive nature; and the second syllable suggests a field, an extent, within which the interaction is operative. It is clearly an 'extent' very different from denotation. It is yet more directive than mere suggestion is. The *Spielraum* idea, I suggest, makes quite clear why there can be no question of asking for literal translations of interaction-metaphors (unlike

---

[4]"Creativity in Language", *Philosophy Today*, vol. 17 Summer Issue, 1973.
[5]*Models and Metaphors*, Cornell University Press, 1962 ch. 3. Originally published in *Proceedings of the Aristotelian Society*, 55 (1954), pp. 273-94.
[6]*Ibid.*, p. 44.
[7]*Ibid.*, p. 45.

in the case of most substitution-metaphors and comparison-metaphors). How does the notion of *Spielraum* tie in with Black's mention of a 'system' of implications? It brings out, I think, the point that systems are not ready to hand, also that interacting systems themselves generate a kind of loose-textured system. As he himself recognises, the reader may be required to use "a special system established for the purpose in hand". To fail to see the point of the metaphor is then presumably to be unable to operate the system. Now the ways in which the failure may take place involve all the ways in which a breakdown of cognition can came about e.g. not seeing the similitude which guided the choice of the metaphor, not seeing which aspects of the 'system' have been selected, not "getting" the emphasis intended and so on. But, if everything clicks, then the reader gains an insight, that is, something of cognitive weight is communicated. Understandably, whenever two systems of impiications interact (I am not speaking of logic here, this should be clear) some of the interactions are more 'important' than others. Now one way of misunderstanding the 'point' of the metaphor is to single out the peripheral interactions. Although an interaction-metaphor cannot be spelt out in a literal way, if it is a 'good' or 'appropriate' metaphor its 'reverberations' present themselves in a way so as to intensify its cognitive content.

The cognitive aspects of certain metaphors are brought out further in Black's more recent work on the subject.[8] In this paper he introduces the notions of 'emphasis' and 'resonance'. Highly emphatic metaphors, he says (those which are not expendable, ornamental etc.) "tend to be highly resonant"[9] (they support a high degree of implicative elaboration). The producers of such metaphors "need the receiver's cooperation in perceiving what lies behind the words used". This way of putting it is reminiscent of the classic formulation of the hermeneutic circle. A metaphorical statement 'works' because of something "produced in the minds of the speaker and hearer".[10] A 'creative response' is called for from the reader. Black in this new treatment ties up more closely the notion of model and metaphor, something also recognised by Mary Hesse. A metaphor's 'focus', Black says, (cf. its 'frame') induces a 'projection' of a secondary system. What projection means is elucidated by 'analogue-model' and 'seeing as'. More challenging, however, is what he says about whether or not metaphors are 'creative'. He suggests that "a metaphorical statement can sometimes generate new knowledge and insight, by *changing* relationships between the things designated (the principal and subsidiary subjects)", and this suggestion has given rise to considerable dismay in certain circles. To understand what he means we need to bear in mind his earlier reference to "rich correspondences, interrelations, and analogies of domains conventionally

---

[8]"More about Metaphor", *Dialectica*, Vol. 31, No. 3-4 (1977).
[9]*Ibid.*, p. 440.
[10]*Ibid.*, p. 442.

separated".[11] Thanks to work in philosophy of science, even stubborn realists are now used to thinking of facts as being theory-laden. Things are seen in certain perspectives. Likewise, "some metaphors enable us to see aspects of reality that the metaphor's production helps to constitute".[12] Metaphors, he continues, can "sometimes function as cognitive instruments through which their users can achieve novel views of a domain of reference".

It would also seem that his view would take in the possibility of opening up a *new* domain of reference and also now relations between *different* domains of reference. But are metaphorical statements related to the facts, to "what is"? His answer here is that indispensable metaphors are not fictions (as Oakeshott thinks), but *show* how things are (cf. charts and maps, graphs, pictorial diagrams, photographs, realistic paintings). They have a 'representational' aspect. At this point he seems to me to retreat to a position (especially through his reference to the cognitive devices of charts etc.) wherein lurks a strong sense of correspondence, whereas up to this point he has been, rightly, thinking of metaphor as an *instrument*. The comparison with *models* is more productive. A model is not a map but a speculative instrument. A metaphor is more than an aid, but I should say, its function is not so much representational, as presentational.

Many matters still remain for analysis. First of all there is the prime distinction between the literal and the metaphoric. We need not polarise these unduly. And yet although "we know very well what is meant by" literality it is not so easy to *say* what we mean. The literal is supposed to be unproblematic and to need no further analysis. But it is easy to slip into thinking of the literal as a paradigm (philosophers who set great store by description tend to do this) and this move seems unwarranted. A literal statement need not be exhaustive, nor even unambiguous. No doubt some literal statements e.g. about wolves, pheasants etc. may be unproblematic. But the man who reports to the doctor that he has a pain in his leg may still have to be questioned further, in cases where (as is the case in some languages) the word for 'leg' is also the word for 'foot'. Ordinary language is often inadequate, and literality is often inadequate. But is it this inadequacy which induces us to use metaphor, and if so, how does metaphor help? There are even cases, perhaps, where a term can be used both literally and metaphorically, odd though this may seem. For example, to say that man is born free but nonetheless everywhere he is in chains includes cases where he actually is in chains (cf. the sort of cases reported by Amnesty International) and also the cases where the 'chains' are metaphoric e.g. poverty, ignorance etc. A similar sort of thing is found in references in classical Indian systems of philosophy to bondage. Let us examine this particular example. If I say to the Advaitin, "Of course you do not mean that we are

---

[11] *Ibid.*, p. 448.
[12] *Ibid.*, p. 454.

literally in bondage", he might reply, "Of course I mean that this is a universal human condition." The boundary between literal and metaphoric seems to have been crossed. Being in bonds in a prison will not be *contrasted* with being in bondage in some overriding sense, but be regarded as an instantiation of it.

There is another peculiarity about literality if we accept the interaction view of metaphor. Even literal expressions are understood in part in virtue of the associated ideas carried by the system they describe and this is a feature which applies to metaphoric expressions too. Interaction suggests a two-way traffic. Another way of putting this question of the impact of the metaphoric on the literal is to say that metaphor does not "leave things as they were". Ah, it may be objected, we should not confuse shift in the connotation of literal description with "changes in reality". At this point a pre-Kantian theory of knowledge rears its head. Winifred Nowottny remarks:[13] "Current criticism often takes metaphor *au grand sérieux*, as a peephole on the nature of transcendental reality, a prime means by which the imagination can see into the life of things." She goes on to say that this attitude "makes it difficult to see the working of those metaphors which deliberately emphasize the frame, offering themselves, as deliberate fabrications, as a prime means of seeing into the life not of things but of the creative human consciousness, framer of its own world." Is it possible to separate seeing into the "life of things" from "the creative human consciousness"? Surely not. The word fabrication unfortunately calls up the sort of associations roused by Prichard's use of the word 'manufacture' in his scathing criticism of Kant's theory of synthesis. The etymological root is, however, innocuous, linked as it is with man as *homo faber*. A new and insightful linguistic expression in a meaningful sense genuinely "makes all things new". Metaphorical discourse finds its rightful place in the quest for intelligibility. It is both a tool of insight and stems from insight. This should not be surprising in view of the original source of the whole discussion about metaphor, Aristotle's grounding of it on the perception of similitude. This is not to deny something also which is an indispensable condition of a metaphor's being *understood*, its dependence on what the hearer of the metaphor already knows. This point is partly taken care of by Black's mention of associated commonplaces, but not altogether so. We seem to need the concept of interlocking "domains" of reference, for it is this that makes possible the shifts of meaning which impel discourse on its way. Here we come across the tremendous variety of operations that thinking involves.

The subject has been neglected by philosophers in no small part thanks to the formalisation of logic that reached its climax in this century. The nineteenth century bequeathed two models for the analysis of thinking – the atomistic, which derived from the "mental chemistry" approach of seventeenth-century thinkers, and the teleological, based on idealist conviction that the *judgement*

---

[13] *The Language Poets use*, (London, Athlone Press, 1962), p. 89.

and not the atomistic 'idea' was both the unit and the vehicle of thought. A third model was later provided by William James with his notion of the stream of consciousness. It was a notion which in itself was metaphoric, and he explicated it by the use of further metaphors. "Like a bird's life, it seems to be made of an alternation of flights and perchings. The rhythm of language expressed this, where every thought is expressed in a sentence, and every sentence closed by a period. The resting places are usually occupied by sensorial imaginations of some sort, whose peculiarity is that they can be held before the mind for an indefinite time, and contemplated without changing; the places of flight are filled with thoughts of relations static and dynamic, that for the most part obtain between the matters contemplated in the periods of comparative rest."[14] He goes on to call the resting-places substantive parts and the places of flight transitive parts of the stream of thought, further to maintain that no language can do justice to the shadings of relation (his own language) within the stream of consciousness.

All this is subjected to interesting criticism by Waismann, who from the standpoint of the logician, could detect a misunderstanding of the working of language in James' understanding of 'and', and 'if' in terms of elusive and 'transitive' feelings.[15] James' was a pioneering venture in attempting to *describe* the dynamism of thought. Waismann is surely right in insisting that dynamism does not require incessant flux. One can be absorbed, one can be stuck, one can hover to and fro between alternatives, one can 'jump' (whether to conclusions or otherwise). Sometimes words go ahead of thought, where, say, an argument leads in a somewhat verbalistic manner to something unacceptable, and we have to retrace our steps. On other occasions the opposite occurs and thought leaps ahead before our words are able to catch up with it. The latter of course is not admitted by those who equate thinking with the use of language.

Once the diversity of the operations of thought is admitted the way is open for avoiding the Scylla of imagism and the Charybdis of pure logic. It is precisely this intermediate channel that the analysis of metaphoric discourse explores. Metaphor is obviously not the only instrument which elucidates the dynamism of thought (mathematical thinking, for example, operates in a different way, although if a metaphor is analogous to a model, it is *akin* to the apparatus which, as Plato saw, *dianoia* uses), but it seems to open up a kind of aperture which enables discourse and it is for this reason that it is of philosophical importance. When the idealists protested against the identification of thought, especially philosophical thought, with linear argument, they were protesting against identifying thought with the serial progression from one concept to another. Discourse grows in no small part

---

[14] *The Principles of Psychology*, i., 243-6 (London, 1890).

[15] There is something equally odd about Frege's treatment of "tone" (Färbung) in terms of mental images.

through the *amplification* of concepts. It is perhaps not a coincidence that Kant understood synthesis in terms of an amplificatory operation without which we would be left with a mere explicatory teasing out of the implications of our concepts. His treatment of the Ideas of Pure Reason gives the outlines of some of the leading 'targets' which thought seeks to reach, but it needs to be matched by an analysis of the strategies of thought which seek to get us there. These strategies can be spoken of as "misemployment of the categories" only so long as philosophical thinking sets itself up as being as scientific (and precisely in the same way) as the natural sciences are.

Once this claim is given up, philosophic discourse can be seen as free to employ strategies like the metaphor in the service of an impulse which strives for intelligibility through the very interlocking of domains of which our experience informs us. It may not get us off the ground, so to speak, but it can be seen as no less 'cosmological' than the route taken by those in the classical tradition who employed analogy. It is through the very overlapping character of domains of experience that we learn 'more'. What at one level seems to be a question of transfer between different semantic fields acquires a further import and is seen to be intimately related to the self-conscious exploration of the texture of experience in and through the coining of modes of expression which can give adequate voice to it. What we explore in an examination of the language of philosophy is very much concerned with the 'between' – what lies between perplexity and the ways that thought adopts to extricate itself from it, what lies between experience and its articulation. The language of philosophy, in other words, is concerned with the link, the path, between question and answer, with what determines the relative 'fit' or otherwise of our temporary 'resting-places' (in James' phrase), with *discourse* in so far as this is not a completed product but which is in the making, something which lays bare the working of thought. The creation of meaningful discourse enlists all our psychical energies and draws on the total resources of language. To deny this would be to trivialise philosophy in a manner which would be not only unwarranted, but unforgivable, amounting as this would, to turning one's back on the entire history of philosophical endeavour. Now if it is philosophical discourse which is the subject-matter of our exploration, it is clear that *concepts* are not the only feature of its texture. What we are in search of is the key to a nexus which brings about intelligibility, and which amounts to discovery. Metaphoric discourse, so far, we have seen as an important generator of meaning, calling upon what we already know, but using this to extend our understanding of the interrelationship of various domains of reference. We have still to examine the cognitive weight of metaphoric discourse and its claim to bring about 'new' insight.

The epistemological consideration with which to begin, I think, is the fact that an extension of knowledge bears a relation to what we already know. It is for this reason that we think it proper, on occasion, to speak of the 'growth' of knowledge. Now those who speak of creativity tend to stress the novelty of the product which issues from creative activity. There is, for example, often a distinction made between 'creative' writing and presumably non-creative writing, a distinction to which those engaged in the latter, quite rightly, object. A good biography, no less than a 'good' poem (I have to beg the question as to what 'good' means here) surely enables us to see things in a new way (in this case, the character who is the subject of the biography, the other characters, the situations, with which he was involved etc.) no less than does the lyric poem which would be generally recognised to be a piece of creative writing. The problem about the metaphysical concept of creativity is how to provide a *link* between the old and the new. Talk of spontaneity seems to provide the needed contrast with determination by antecedents or the pull of a *telos*. But for there to be *no* continuity whatsoever between the old and the new, what is known and the breakthrough of discovery, would make it unintelligible, and, moreover, deprive thought of its essential pabulum.

The literature relating to the alleged creativity of metaphorical discourse ranges between regarding metaphors as fictions to looking on them as generating a new reality which may even throw up actuality in an unfavourable light. Oakeshott is at one end of the spectrum in regarding "poetic imagining" (as in so-called indispensable metaphors) as dealing with 'fictions' which are in no way "contributions to an enquiry into the nature of the real world".[16] Black's earlier statement[17] on this question is guarded. He says: "It would be more illuminating in some of these cases (i.e., of metaphors imputing similarities, difficult to discern otherwise) to say that it formulates some similarity antecedently existing." This is merely a *suggestion*, and which does not actually advocate anything. So Black is not affected by the criticism that it is wrong to conflate creation of an effect in the mind of the hearer or reader with creation of a similarity between the principal and subsidiary subject. Black takes the view in his later paper (in *Dialectica*) that "some metaphors enable us to see aspects of reality that the metaphor's production helps to constitute". He ties this in neatly with the linguistic turn which sees the world as a world "under a certain description". A world under a certain description is seen from a certain perspective. And he concludes that "some metaphors can create such a perspective".[18] We are perhaps not debarred from linking the possibility of new perspectives with that intellectual subsoil (partly individual and partly belonging to a cultural continuum) to which Waismann draw attention. We can also perhaps add the point that the difference between the literal and the metaphoric can be seen as a difference between description and re-description.

---

[16] M. Oakeshott, *The Voice of Poetry in the Conversation of Mankind*, London, Bowes and Bowes, 1959, p. 45–6.

[17] "Metaphor" in *Models and Metaphors*, ch. 3.

[18] *Dialectica*, Vol. 31, No. 3-4 (1977), p. 454.

Re-description becomes necessary as phenomena change and our ways of cognizing them change.

Black's use of the word perspective can be set alongside that of Kenneth Burke. The latter writes: "Metaphor is a device for seeing something *in terms of something else*....A metaphor tells us something about one character seen from the point of view of another character. And to consider A from the point of view of B is, of course, to use B as a perspective on A."[19] The point at issue is whether it is B that provides the perspective or "considering A from the point of view of B" that provides the perspective. The latter is surely the case. The metaphor sets in operation something which is not a mere Blik (the word perspective may unfortunately suggest this) but which generates a whole network of meanings, a genuinely *new* domain of reference. That this generating includes further metaphor is not surprising. Wheelwright's suggestion that only 'fluid language' is able to work in this way is useful. If we take this fluidity seriously then the meaning "aimed at"[20] cannot be independent of the meanings which carry the movement of thought. Whereas no one who tends towards vitalism would object to this. Critics who are afraid of the naturalist bogey may baulk at this point.

Among other writers who have written on metaphor (and they are legion) Paul Ricoeur's work is of special interest for the way in which he combines semantic and non-semantic considerations, ties in metaphor with the working of imagination (more in the style of German writers on the theme) and regards them as fictions which have a non-heuristic use. His paper on "Creativity in language" first presented in 1972[21] is concerned initially with distinguishing between metaphoric discourse and ordinary and scientific language. He detects an "infinite character" in semantic entities for the following reason: "Discourse is infinite because sentences are events, because they have a speaker and a hearer, because they have meanings, and because they have reference." He continues: "With the event comes the openness of temporality, with the speaker and hearer the depth of individual fields of experience, with meaning the limitlessness of the thinkable, and with references the inexhaustibility of the world itself." He regards scientific language as a language which seeks to eradicate polysemy. But if metaphor is a creative use of polysemy, as he maintains, and if metaphoric discourse and model-using are analogous, the natural sciences (as distinct from the pure disciplines of mathematics and logic) may not be, or need to be, entirely free from polysemy. This consideration, however,

---

[19] Quoted by Paul Henle in "Metaphor", in *Language, Thought and Culture* ed. by Henle, 1958, p. 192.

[20] A phrase used by Jacques Derrida, "White Mythology" trans. F.C.T. Moore, *New Literary History*, 6 (1974), 1:29.

[21] Delivered as a lecture at the Fifth Lexington Conference on Pure and Applied Phenomenology at the Veterans' Administration Hospital in Lexington, Kentucky. Translated in *Philosophy Today*, Vol. 17, Summer issue, 1973, pp. 97-111.

is not pertinent to the main direction of the paper. Ricoeur wishes to link the informative character of metaphoric discourse with its "creative dimension". We are here dealing with the novel metaphor, one which no longer relies on the previous range of commonplaces at our disposal, but where we "create a new framework of connotation which exists only in the actual act of predication".

This involves paradoxes. Metaphor is both the object of insight and the vehicle which brings it about. The very copula too conveys a paradox, sameness and difference, is and is not. Metaphor blurs[22] conceptual boundaries in the interest of detecting new similarities. This might suggest that "the dynamics of thought which breaks through previous categorization is the same as the one which generated all classifications". The question that might arise, however, is whether the dynamism of thinking which establishes logical boundaries is akin to the dynamism which reallocates them, and reallocates, moreover, in a way very different from classification as such. Frege speaks clearly on this: "An indeterminate concept must correspond to a district whose boundary lines were not sharply drawn but lost themselves here and there in the surrounding country. This would not really be a district at all and similarly a concept which is not sharply delimited cannot truly be called a concept. Such vague ideas, though they resemble concepts, cannot be recognised by logic as concepts; it is impossible to draw up exact rules governing them."[23] Ironically enough the point is made through the use of a metaphor! Using a different metaphor, Wheelwright makes the opposite point: "If reality is largely fluid and half-paradoxical, steel nets are not the best instruments for taking samples of it."[24] One way of dealing with this tangle is not to think of the metaphor as a sort of concept. The metaphor presents an intersection of meanings, which is not the same as the joint affirmation of concepts. Ricoeur, however, is right in searching for some kind of common structure, or even continuity, between the strategies of thought which lead to conceptualisation of a classificatory kind (where what Black calls 'resonance' is underplayed) and those which issue in metaphoric discourse. To do otherwise would be to revert to the dichotomy between rational and irrational encouraged by eighteenth-century faculty psychology, but for which there is scarce warrant today.

Ricoeur's next move is to look at imagination "as the place of nascent meanings and categories", taking a cue from the Kant of the Schematism. To go into this would involve examining the role of the pre-conceptual in thinking. Ricoeur tends to stress the interplay between sameness and difference in metaphoric discourse. But no less important is the interplay between abstract and concrete, for metaphor enables us to *embody* our thinking, and metaphor individualises[25] in an idiosyncratic way. This function of metaphor is polar to

---

[22]Turbayne speaks of category-fusion rather than of blurring.
[23]*Grundgesetze der Arithmetik*, ii. 69 (Jena, 1893).
[24]*Metaphor and Reality,* Bloomington, 1967, p. 128.
[25]This is also recognised by Hedwig Konrad in her *Étude sur la métaphore*, Paris, Lavergne, 1939.

the function which likens it to classification. It would be mistaken, perhaps, to identify this individualising function with the iconic element in all cases. In the case of poetic metaphor, yes. But good prose can accommodate plenty of metaphors where we are not called upon to *dwell* on them, to enjoy them, but to follow the *what* which is being said. However, the role of imagination is taken up for discussion at a later stage, in his book on metaphor.

The paper concludes with the idea of metaphors as "heuristic fictions". This idea is the bridge between models in science and metaphors in poetry. A creative fiction enables its user to redescribe. Here his point is more or less the same as Black's reference to new perspectives. Reality redescribed is "novel reality". In his major book on the subject,[26] Ricoeur speaks more overtly of the 'power' that heuristic fictions have. Metaphor has its own order. He now tends to find its dynamism in the *replacing* of logical order. The French title of the original edition expresses better than does the English the essential liveliness of metaphor. He goes further on the track of rooting the emergence of metaphor. Michel Le Guern has spoken of living metaphor as "image-triggering".[27] But does this suggest that metaphor, like Kant's "Schema" provides rules for the "production" of images? Ricoeur's suggestion is helpful in this regard: "The only way to approach the problem of imagination from the perspective of a semantic theory, that is to say on a verbal plane, is to begin with productive imagination in the Kantian sense....Treated as a schema, the image presents a verbal dimension; before being the gathering-point of faded perceptions, it is that of emerging meanings."[28] Now, is speech an aura surrounding the image or vice versa? Gaston Bachelard says that the image is an aura surrounding speech.[29] Another alternative is to find in the image the sensuous articulation of what metaphor provides at the verbal level. The two orders of articulation in this way represent something stressed by Kant, the indispensability of sense and understanding to each other. Recast in terms of varied articulations this emerges as the indispensability of the figurative and the non-figurative to each other once we are outside the domains of mathematics and logic. This would also explain why those who are otherwise unsympathetic to figurative expressions such as Kant and Frege, nevertheless find themselves using them. The indispensability can be looked at diversely. One way is to find in this a *limitation* of reason. Another way is to see it as an important vehicle whereby, through varying modes of transfers of meaning, thought is lent wings. The latter metaphor is perhaps, on second thoughts, unfortunate. To enable us to proceed horizontally, along the ground, is no doubt no less important a way in which metaphor serves us, and one of the legitimate roles of the Ideas,

---

[26] *The Rule of Metaphor*, Routledge and Kegan Paul, 1978 (Translated from *La Metaphore vive*, 1975).
[27] *Sémantique de la metaphore et de la metonymie*, Paris, Larousse, 1973.
[28] *Ibid.*, p. 199.
[29] Vide *The Poetics of Space*, trans. Maria Jolas, Boston, Beacon, 1969.

according to Kant, was to guide, through overarching regulative principles, the inductive exploration of nature. The issue is posed for us quite clearly by Kant, whether non-categorial concepts can do more for us than this (in his own view, of course, they also had a crucial part to play in connection with the moral consciousness).

So far the implicit dialogue with Kant that surfaces from time to time in this chapter has resulted in something like the following. First, the productive imagination seems to have a role beyond what Kant allots it in the Schematism. If there is a blurring of boundaries between sense and understanding in the subjective deduction of the categories there seems something analogous to this where imagination and reason are concerned. The reason why such an idea is quite foreign to Kant is that he is classical enough in temperament to associate the essential metaphysical impulse with a disposition to go *beyond* the sensible and to link imagination with *sense* rather than with reason. Secondly, the strange conflation of imagination and reason that seems to be at work in the more adventurous reaches of thought seems to issue in something which may not be strictly either constitutive or regulative. One reason for this is that the operative factors are thrown up by experience itself, that is, their pedigree seems thoroughly empirical; and yet, to grasp them requires something more than more perceptual thinking. So also, it could be pointed out, scientific thinking can be said to outpace perceptual thinking. But scientific thinking is firmly oriented towards the discovery of law. Here again we cannot but concede, with Kant, that the metaphysical disposition is directed not towards the discovery of law but towards *totality* (rather than unity), whatever we may find this means. There is, in other words, amidst the multiform ways in which we reflect on our experience, a disposition to organise our efforts to understand through an outreach *other* than the rule-seeking adventure of the scientific mind. But how is such totality to be found? What is set us as a task is undoubtedly a direction in which to proceed, a goal which becomes clearer as we spell out the multiform relations in which discourse consists. The background context of this is surely 'the manifold'. Kant has influenced modern thinking sufficiently for us to allow that the manifold cannot be specified or identified at all without the categorial frameworks we use. That is, we cannot, in realist fashion, take our point of departure from the manifold per se.

The third point concerns possibility. And here we may need to say something like this. In addition to the conditions of the possibility of experience (and we may not necessarily agree with Kant's once-and-for-all listing of what these are) *experience itself* is full of possibilities. I can compare X with Y or with Z and so on ad infinitum. What to one man appears as analogous to a beating of wings in empty space appears to another as a vision of the sun, or to yet another as a still and uncharacterisable moment of illumination. Our experience is full and rich enough to enable us not only to juxtapose in thought what is not juxtaposed in nature, but to find in so doing a source of insight. We find here, it could be suggested, a new meaning of the 'conceivable', and one to which etymology adds resonance – a germinal insight which is capable of growth. The process involved is not linear so much as expansive, a further fulfilling and rippling out from a central insight. This central something is misnamed 'concept' if by concept we mean 'the bounded'. If it sounds paradoxical to speak of a mode of conceivability which does not deal with concepts we may speak instead of intelligibility, or of foci of meaning. A horizon is always seen *from* a standpoint. But the horizon itself is essentially moving. It moves as we move. The *possibility* of metaphorical discourse is grounded on the inexhaustible variations of experience, and the unusual figurative expression sets in motion stirrings of accumulated experience with their open-ended possibilities of further development, so that a new insight may ensue.

The fourth point in our implicit dialogue with Kant is to distinguish what has been said just now from something of which Kant was always highly suspicious, the claim to an 'intellectual intuition'. Claim to the latter was a natural accompaniment of an ontological view of the universe where the intellect was cast for a penetrative role rather than a relational one. It was essentially a theological model in that the belief that man can intuit the natures of things went hand in hand with the assumption of rationality 'located' in three plates, the mind of God, the mind of man and the nature of things. Once Hume and Kant had shown that this model was undemonstrable, the ground was cut from beneath the feet of those who spoke of intellectual intuition. The intelligible, henceforth, for epistemologists, was to be seen in terms of *relations* between particulars rather than in terms of particulars whose essential nature could be made manifest in a single act of intuition. From this it should be clear that what we have been suggesting is not akin to the ontologist's claim to an intellectual intuition. For one thing, the process involved has been found to be not purely intellectual at all, sensibility and imagination being intimately caught up in it. And the insight gained is not a punctual intuition, a clear and distinct *terminus*, so much as a vista to be explored, a continuing invitation to go in a certain direction. Along with this, admittedly, there can be a sense of *limit*, but limit in the sense of what is *appropriate*, limit in the sense of what the *Spielraum* of the new expression is. What writing of quality after all does not hinge on a fine *sense of judgement*? If intuition is an unsuitable term to express all this, no less unsuitable are the terms 'judgement' or 'predication'. We *feel our way in thought*. If metaphoric discourse plays the role it seems to in this feeling one's way then we cannot be said to be groping[30] with mere *concepts*

---

[30] The word Kant uses in Bvii of the Preface to the Second Edition of the *Critique of Pure Reason*. "Herumtappen", suggests going round and round in a purposeless fashion. Cf. the tongue-twister, "In Ulm, um Ulm, und um Ulm herum". A metaphor, however, can provide a certain sense of direction, although nothing which Kant would have credited with the role of "determination", which, for him, depends invariably on *judgement*.

when we venture beyond the "bounds" of perceptual thought. Should we regard metaphoric discourse as symptomatic of a loss of ontology or does it not, perhaps, in a subtle way, itself possess ontological weight? We need next to close in on this question by looking more specifically at metaphors used in philosophical discourse.

CHAPTER V

Metaphor and Philosophical Discourse

A study of the history of philosophy shows that the nerve of philosophical discourse is argument. To say this, however, does not open magic doors for the same can be said of mathematics, of legal discourse, and, to take a more contemporary example, the computerised diagnosis used in up to date hospitals. There are various *types* of argument used by philosophers, and philosophers, especially in recent years, have devoted a lot of attention to plotting the various ways these arguments 'work', and the extent to which they *do* work. Philosophical arguments arise in the attempt to answer questions of special kinds. And yet what makes us decide that a particular 'answer' satisfactorily *fits* a philosophical question? The conclusions to which philosophical arguments lead often disconcert us. The dogmatist, the sceptic, and the solipsist, provide, in their turn, evidence for the view that arguments can be dangerous things. Later on it will be necessary to return to the theme of argument when we pull together the issues that are emerging as we go along, the involvement of reason with imagination, the range of linguistic imagination, the credentials of description. Our immediate purpose is with the place of metaphor in philosophical discourse. To some minds this may seem either an irrelevant task ("the point is the *argument*, not the metaphor") or a misguided one. If we think of metaphor as "the most conspicuous point of contact between meaning and poetry"[1] this need not prevent us from recognising its role in philosophy. For *not* to recognise it is to shut one's eyes to something which is writ large in the history of philosophy. Even philosophers who have been attached to definitions have freely used metaphors. Generalised world views, models, and specific arguments have so often centred on metaphors, and this should tell us something about the nature of the philosophical impulse and the vehicle of philosophical thought, to say nothing of the language of philosophy.

It is necessary, perhaps, at this stage, to take the measure of those considerations which have led to a neglect of the metaphorical and to the assumption that there is something rock-bottom about literality. Much water has flowed under philosophical bridges since the positivists' threefold division

---

[1]*Poetic Diction*, Owen Barfield, p. 63.

of sentences into the literally significant, the valid and the nonsensical. The quest for literal significance was tied up no doubt with a praiseworthy concern for the informative, but the idea that termini could be found in the shape of theory-free data was subsequently found to be all too simplistic. The matter was not one which only philosophers busied themselves with by any means. Literary critics and linguists were very much in the picture, although, with perhaps the distinguished exception of I.A. Richards, each set of practitioners imagined that they alone were on the job. There was a certain logic about saying that there could hardly be a metaphorical use of a certain expression unless there were a literal use to contrast it with. In some quarters the literal uses were taken as standards and metaphorical ones as deviations. Others found dead metaphors all over the place. Linguistic anthropology seemed to give the lie to the view that block language was primitive, and along with this, nouns lost the pride of place which some grammarians and ontologists had given them. The evidence was all in favour of the fluidity of primitive language and a blurring of boundaries between literal and metaphorical. If there be a rock-bottom it is the total relation which man bears to his environment (including in this the social dimension), where man finds it natural to speak figuratively because his consciousness is above all a symbolising consciousness. This symbolising can be illustrated from the sign left behind for other dwellers in the forest, the imitative calls made during hunting, gestures of warning, ritual dances, right through to the well-turned phrase and metaphor, the speculative flight embodied in a metaphysical system. It would have been strange had it been otherwise. To realise that figurative expression is natural to man is, for the philosopher, to see a way out of being forced to choose between correspondence and coherence. Thought is not called upon to 'reflect' anything that is alien to it. We do not start with one-to-one correspondences, but with orientations in a world which is bone of our bone, where the sound of the human voice chimes in with the sound of the waterfall, the crackle of twig underfoot, and the cry of wild creatures in the forest. In the highest flights of speculative thought we do not lose our link with the sensible. The wholes we construct are welded through the figurations of 'harmony' and 'theme' which in turn are cashable in terms of colour and sound.

When Locke wrote in Book IV of his *Essay* that all things were retainers to other parts of nature he was replacing a philosophy of relational properties for a metaphysic of discrete substances. Something analogous can be said of speech. Anything that we say is retainer to other things said. This is the source of those transfers of expression that bring about new insight. The symbolising consciousness is at home in a world which houses both affinities and differences and where each note, each moment, has resonances. Man's creative endeavours come about through a fertile friction of ideas, a friction which neither mechanism nor teleology can 'explain'.

But what of etymology in all this? Etymology can be a good corrective to reliance on current usage. Current usages trail clouds of previous usages. This does not mean that many are not dropped on the way. They obviously are. But etymology should not blind us to the possibility of new usages and such new usages can be invented by any of the trail-blazing symbolisers – scientists, poets and philosophers.

To say that figurative expression is natural to man not only protects us from too easy acquiescence in the dichotomies literal/metaphoric, real/fictional, but offers us a fourth alternative to three familiar models for relating consciousness and the world, the net, the penetrative, and the reflective models. We neither cast once-for-all meshes, wrest once-for-all essences, nor mirror once-for-all realities. We constantly change gear, swop lenses and if there is anything rock-bottom it is the fact that we do all this. So the search for 'the given', for 'what is said', for the literal, for the lowest common measure, is mistaken. Nor do we need to posit any such stratum in order to make sense of the metaphorical. Our metaphor-making, our model-constructing, is not the work of fancy but the work of what is most real of all – the symbolising consciousness of man, a consciousness which operates through shifts, transfers, leaps, overlaps and criss-crossing movements. Since this is so, linear discourse appears as a very special conquest on the part of man – neither superior nor inferior, but something carved out of a medium to which it is not immediately hospitable. There are those who, perhaps on this account, associate the use of metaphor with what is intrinsically *difficult*. When thought comes to a halt, when the material is dense and complex, then metaphor-making comes to our aid. The objection to putting it like this is that it reduces metaphor to a kind of interlude after which linear thinking again comes into full operation. An opposite extreme is to regard metaphor as a kind of protection against the strait-jacket of logic. Gomperz writes of Parmenides. "...his mind was imaginative and poetical, and (he) was thus protected from the logical consequences of his premises."[2] A different and very unexpected admission of the crucial role of metaphor is made by A.J. Ayer in writing about Wittgenstein: "The turning point was the shift in Wittgenstein's philosophy, from the metaphor of treating words as pictures to the metaphor of treating words as tools."[3]

I do not myself think we need to plump for any one of these radical positions with respect to metaphors in philosophical writing. Metaphor does not just plug a gap, not does it add complexity to complexity. Metaphor-making, and this must be stressed, need not be regarded as polar to strict argument, for as I shall hope to show, metaphor can enter into the very nerve of argument, and (to mix the metaphor) propel it on its way. Sometimes a whole change in mode of philosophising is epitomised in a basic change in metaphor, as in the example

---

[2]*The Greek Thinkers*, Vol. I, Laurie Magnus, trans. (New York, 1908), p. 178.
[3]Vide Ch. on "Philosophy and Language" in *The Concept of a Person and Other Essays.*

given by Ayer. But we would be on the wrong track if we expect of all metaphors in philosophy that they should be as radical as this.

This provides an introduction to my reaction to the work of two people who have written specifically (but differently) on the subject of metaphors in philosophy, S.C. Pepper and C.M. Turbayne. Pepper in his book *World-Hypotheses* talks about how metaphysical systems arise from a basic analogy or root metaphor. The philosopher "pitches upon some area of common-sense fact and tries if he cannot understand other areas in terms of this one....A list of its structural characteristics becomes his basic concepts of explanation and description....Since the basic analogy or root metaphor normally (and probably at least in part necessarily) arises out of common-sense, a great deal of development and refinement of a set of categories is required if they are to provide adequate for a hypothesis of unlimited scope."[4] He goes on to classify the use of fictions in rational discourse into four: mechanism, formism, organicism, and contextualism. He shows in a very interesting way how an initial insight develops into an over-arching analogue and how the root metaphor serves to organise other metaphors into networks. This is a salutary antidote to looking on individual metaphors in a pointilliste way. But any attempt to found a typology always faces the challenge of types left out, unclassifiables, mixed cases and so on. Some metaphors *are* more radical than others in the sense that they serve as models, and generate other metaphors. If we use the word hypothesis, moreover, as Pepper does, we are reminded of the point that over-arching hypotheses, unlike the working scientists' hypotheses, cannot be verified or falsified. That a root metaphor or model may well be implicit or submerged in a philosopher's thought is also a point well made. To uncover the root metaphor can be to gain further understanding of a philosopher's overall position and those who *have* such a position are no doubt hedgehogs rather than foxes. To be aware that there are alternative root metaphors can act as a prophylactic against dogmatism, and even against scepticism. Pepper's plotting of the map of the speculative instruments of the metaphysician came at a time when positivist criticism of metaphysics (*and* over-simplifications in philosophy of science) needed rebuttal. Rooting a metaphysical model in an "area of common sense fact", moreover, provided a certain empirical anchorage for metaphysical thinking at a time when it was assumed in fashionable circles that the metaphysician had none. But when all this is said, the history of ideas does not support the particular classification that Pepper makes, nor, in principle, can any classification *be* made, for no limit can be set to the cues the philosopher may get from experience, the metaphors which may appear dominant and archetypal for him. Furthermore, some of the transfers which set a metaphysical system on its way are mis-described as metaphorical. A philosopher often imports concepts from other

---

[4]University of California Press, 1942, pp. 91-92.

disciplines. Aristotle imported concepts from biology, Hobbes from chemistry, and Berkeley from psychology. Spinoza was inspired mainly by logic and geometry in so far as the form of his thought is concerned. We may be ill advised to regard all such importations as metaphorical transfers.

Whereas the mainspring of Pepper's book is the impulse to detect and classify, Turbayne[5] seems chiefly concerned to warn us. He notes that Gilbert Ryle's definition of a category mistake as the taking of facts as if they belong to one sort of category when they actually belong to another can be taken as a definition of metaphor. A metaphor should not be taken literally, says Turbayne. Those who use metaphors he calls "sort-crossers", and victims of metaphor are "sort-trespassers". In the course of his argument he tries to make out that Descartes and Newton can be classed in the latter category. They are alleged to have fallen victim in three ways. The first is that they took the necessary connection of premises and deduced conclusions to be duplicated in the world of causes and effects. The second is the error of hylopsychism, the attribution to inanimate matter of the properties of living bodies, i.e. force and power. Finally, they identified deduction with computation, making mathematical calculation a defining characteristic of scientific description. All these three amount together, Turbayne says, to the doctrine of mechanism, the view that the world is not *like* a machine, but *is* a machine.

A later piece of writing by Turbayne[6] throws further light on the above piece of analysis. He therein distinguishes between three uses of metaphor by philosophers, first an unsystematic use, secondly, where a metaphor or analogy is extended into a theory or model, and thirdly, where the metaphor is hidden and the comparison is not overtly made. Let us examine each of these in turn. An example of the unsystematic use of metaphors would be Hume's use of the 'bundle', 'stage' and 'republic' metaphors in discussing the identity of the self. When such metaphors are taken together, Turbayne thinks they constitute a mixed metaphor. As a mixed metaphor is usually considered stylistically defective I would prefer to say, of this first kind, that the philosopher is here employing a series of independent metaphors which enable him to close in on what he wishes to convey. The sustained single metaphor is illustrated satisfactorily by Turbayne in Plato's use of the charioteer/wild horses figure in the *Phaedrus* and the comparison of the mind with a political community divided into classes in the *Republic*. The rub comes with the third kind, for Turbayne believes that here we not only have an extended metaphor but a submerged one which has become a 'myth', and which is *believed*. Such myths need to be brought to the surface, he thinks, and this unmasking serves to show up the nature of the conceptual scheme with which we operate. To take a heuristic device literally is to be led into confusion. To explode a myth or

---

[5]Colin Murray Turbayne, *The Myth of Metaphor*, Yale University Press, 1962.

[6]"Metaphors for the Mind" in *Logic & Art*, Essays in honor of Nelson Goodman, Ed. by Richard Rudner and Israel Scheffler. Bobbs-Merrill Co., Inc. 1972.

undress a metaphor is to show that "these sometimes valuable fusions are actually confusions".[7] The thesis is supported by an extended analysis of Berkeley who perhaps exposes himself to multiple lines of attack, J.O. Wisdom also having attempted a different kind of 'unmasking'. But let us return to the comments about Descartes and Newton.

The threefold victimisation to which they are said to have fallen seems to cover rather different kinds of 'mistake', if mistakes they be. The rationalist 'confusion' of logical necessity with causal necessity is ill described in terms of metaphoric transfer. As for hylopsychism, this is hardly a view which can be ascribed to a strict dualist who was keen to point out that *res extensa* was in fact radically *other* than *res cogitans*. To argue *de more geometrico*, moreover, is not the same as making mathematical calculation "a defining characteristic of scientific description". But let us, for the sake of argument, grant that Descartes and Newton operated with the 'metaphor' (or rather 'model') of mechanism. It was a highly successful undertaking and dominated various fields of thought for a period of time which ran into centuries. One can hardly be victimised by something that is successful. Then one and the same 'fusion' cannot be at one time valuable and, at another, a confusion. If a fusion is a deliberate transfer then it is presumably made with one's eyes open, that is, knowing what one is doing, *not* taking it literally and so forth. Are we to suppose that when Descartes spoke of the mind as residing in its body like "a pilot in his ship"[8] he was so misguided as to mean it literally? Surely not. This particular example would qualify for Turbayne's own prescription, the conscious use of a metaphor "with awareness". But there is a proviso. Such a use of metaphor is to be preceded by "an approximate grasp of the literal truth". It is here that we run into difficulty, for the matters which occupy philosophers are those which cannot be talked about through the literal use of language. To hark back to literality as a desirable standard is to hark back to the view that there is a single categorisation of the facts which represents them "as they really are". The idea of a 'wrong categorisation' would indeed seem to presuppose some such paradigmatic categorisation.

Is it not rather the case that reallocations of facts are constantly going on, and when an allocation is 'accepted' it is such only for the time being? The 'facts' take on different aspects as we alter our metaphors. One man's confusion is another's illumination. Metaphors fall into the basket of neither make-believe or belief. Sort-crossing is as familiar in ordinary discourse as it is in philosophical thinking. If this is so, then there *is* no rock-bottom. Our overlapping, interacting, intersecting forms of life are matched by our fluid forms of language. Even particulars (the darlings of new-look ontologies) are and are not what they are. They are certainly not complete and closed. We can but see

---

[7]*The Myth of Metaphor*, pp. 4-5.
[8]*Meditations on First Philosophy* II.

a particular as a multiple cue for multiple interpretations. And one is not *acquainted* with a cue, one does not 'identify' it; one takes it as a point of departure. If this be so, whether it makes sense at all to speak of philosophy as descriptive is something to be taken up later. In the meantime, the examination of metaphors used in philosophical discourse, so far from having a debunking effect, seems to increase our understanding of philosophical viewpoints and it also seems to be the case that philosophers who use them are quite aware of what they are doing.

Whether the choice of metaphor is itself a subterranean operation which has deep and dark aspects will occupy us in due course. The considerations which guide our judgement of whether a metaphor 'fits', is apt or appropriate, helpful or obfuscating, cannot be summarised in a cut and dried manner. It is because this is so that there can be no sharp demarcation between what Turbayne calls sort-crossing and sort-trespassing. In the end, Turbayne (like Russell and Waismann before him) finds the most deeply entrenched pressures come *not* from our adventures in sort-crossing (something which I should say merit bouquets rather than brickbats) but from grammar, and at this point he joins the mainstream of those who paradoxically find in the grammatical structure of the favourite oracle, ordinary language, the source of the mixed bag of failures that some philosophers love to pick over, in short 'confusions' in general.

The rest of this chapter will be devoted to showing how philosophers' metaphors advance the exposition of their viewpoints, and (where appropriate) enter into the texture of their arguments. I shall confine myself to three very different philosophers, Kant, Husserl and Ryle.

There has been occasion to mention more than once earlier in this study the reasons for Kant's exclusion of imagination from the structure of metaphysical thinking, and at the same time to realise how deeply sympathetic he was with the disposition which leads the philosopher to be impatient with categorial thinking and to soar beyond the boundaries which enable us to distinguish between true and false. A meta-critical reflection on his own practice as a philosopher reveals some interesting features about his own use of language and the various strategies which he uses within the framework of his own transcendental approach. It will be found that the philosopher who disapproved of the 'descriptive' physiological method of Locke and the demonstrator's obsession with definitions, did in fact utilise a number of techniques in the course of his identification of the presuppositions of experience.

One can begin first with metaphors of elaboration used not for purposes of diversion or entertainment, but which were germane to a good prose style. Examples of this are found in abundance in Kant's Preface to the second edition of his first *Critique*, beginning with the metaphor of travellers on a journey proceeding towards a destination, and on occasion having to retrace their steps. Travellers who proceed on a sure path are contrasted with those who do not. This is reminiscent of the concept of the pilgrim which was familiar to German Romantic thought. Here the tragic 'hero', misguided and hitherto disappointed in his journey, is none other than the metaphysician. Metaphors follow thick as leaves in Vallombrosa: 'nature's leading strings', 'question and answer', 'approaching nature', 'pupil and teacher'. Just as the judge is not passive before his witness, but asks leading questions (this was the practice in the courts of Kant's day), so likewise the mind is not a blank tablet on which experience writes, but itself formulates questions for nature to answer. These are examples of completely successful metaphors, where there is no ambiguity and where the writer himself delimits precisely the range of implications he wishes to call into play. These particular metaphors are linked together by the role they share in explicating what could be called a model – the overarching model of the "Copernican Revolution". Kant himself refers to the latter as a hypothesis. We are to "make trial whether we may not have more success in the tasks of metaphysics, if we suppose that objects must conform to our knowledge".[9] What we would then be doing is to proceed "precisely on the lines of Copernicus' primary hypothesis".[10] The idea of 'modelling' is contained in Kemp Smith's translation: "This method, modelled on that of the student of nature."[11] The original suggests more the idea of 'copy' ("Diese dem Naturforscher nachgeahmte Methode"). In any case to call the 'Copernican Revolution' a model is itself to speak metaphorically. There has been a double transfer. The Copernican Revolution was initially a new model in astronomy. It is astronomy that is the 'original domain'. What was originally a new model in astronomy is now transferred to philosophy. It is clearly neither a philosophical fable (cf. the many fables used by Kierkegaard) nor a literary allegory. It does not have 'explanatory power' as a scientific model has, so much as provide a new perspective which puts a central philosophical problem in a new light, the whole epistemological relation between subject and object. It is also quite different from "examples and other concrete illustrations",[12] of which Kant had a poor opinion, referring to them as the "go-cart of judgement", factors which pull us by the nose. When Kant *does* use examples he is none too successful. His most important one is the appeal to our perception of a house and a moving ship respectively in order to illustrate the difference between subjective and objective succession. His argument can stand (qua argument) without this example and indeed is better off without it. Kant's examples arise almost incidentally in the course of rigorous and logical sequences of arguments.

It is not surprising that a philosopher who strove to make philosophy scientific, and who from the beginning had been professionally concerned with

[9] *Critique of Pure Reason*, Kemp Smith Ed. B XVII.
[10] *Ibid.*, B XVII.
[11] *Ibid.*, B XIX.
[12] *Ibid.*, A XVIII.

many of the sciences, should make frequent reference to scientific concepts. Apart from the leading ideas of hypothesis and experiment, there are, for example, a number of references to geometry, optics and astronomy in the Dialectic. The *focus imaginarius* passage (A 645/B 672/673) and the horizon analogy (A 658/B 686) derive from his interest in optics, the "cone" example from geometry (A 715/B 743), and there is a fairly lengthy reference to the orbits of the planets in A 663/B 691. Although it is generally believed that Kant's departure from ontology made him unsympathetic to analogical thinking, he used quite a few analogies himself and to more effect than his occasional addition of examples here and there.

If an example can go awry, a piece of metaphoric discourse *can* lead to misunderstanding. We need next to examine the way metaphor enters into a very important part of Kant's *Critique* and did in fact make him open to a particular line of attack. Professor Bird, in his book on *Kant's Theory of Knowledge*, has given a very valuable analysis of Prichard's attempted debunking of Kant's theory of synthesis. Much hinges on Prichard's unwillingness to admit that 'construction' can be other than literal, and to grant that Kant used both 'construction' and 'synthesis' in a way peculiarly his own. Prichard's charge of 'manufacture' stems from both this unwillingness and his neglect of Kant's teaching about the "manifold". Bird's discussion is especially interesting for the way he detects metaphors where others had failed to detect any. In Bird's view he uses a "chronological metaphor" in his logical classification of modal terms when he says at B 101: "...We first judge something problematically, then maintain its truth assertorically, and finally affirm it as inseparably united with the understanding."[13] His next examples are perhaps more telling: the famous dictum which starts off the Introduction at B 1 and the statement at B 730: "Thus all human knowledge begins with intuition, proceeds from thence to concepts, and ends with ideas." Any student of Kant, however, should know that Kant is not speaking literally here, for otherwise the distinction between beginning with and arising out of, which is crucial to his transcendental standpoint, could not be made at all.

Bird goes on to point out that the first moment of the threefold synthesis in the Subjective Deduction of the Categories is presented by Kant through the metaphors of 'running through' and 'holding together'. The issue, as I see it in the context of our main theme, concerns, firstly, the extent to which a philosopher, even a rigorous one like Kant, often relies on *not* being taken literally, and secondly, the way in which a mode of presentation can give a handle to unfavourable criticism. It is not only metaphors that can give such a handle. Brand Blanshard pointed out long ago how philosophical style can set up a barrier to understanding. But Kant, foreseeing criticism, had known very well that "A philosophical work cannot be armed at all points, like a

---

[13] Graham Bird, *Kant's Theory of Knowledge*, 1962, p. 9.

mathematical treatise...."[14] Kant's critics are partly answered in the closing passages of the Preface to the second edition of the *Critique of Pure Reason*: "If we take single passages, torn from their contexts, and compare them with one another, apparent contradictions are not likely to be lacking, especially in a work that is written with any freedom of expression."[15] Just as Kant draws a distinction between objects and the mode of our knowledge of objects "in so far as this mode of knowledge is to be possible a priori", we can likewise note how the corpus of a philosopher's work has been shaped by his mode of philosophising. To begin to do this with respect to the language Kant uses (and what I have sketched barely scratches the surface) is to find, perhaps with surprise in view of the rigour with which Kant's philosophy is associated, that he does in fact often write with considerable "freedom of expression."

Let us turn by way of contrast to phenomenology. The language used by the phenomenologist in his philosophical writing shows most noticeably a move away from the strategies of argument. The approach is a quite different one, stemming from a shift from language to speech, a grounding of all saying in the subject and his intentions, and a stress made on the important distinction between meaning-intention and meaning-fulfilment. On Husserl's view, all three of these matters are presented on the basis of phenomenological evidence. What does this amount to? We are invited first to realise that thinking of language as an objectified reified something is very different from seeing it embodied in the communicative situation between speaker and hearer. The starting point of communication is the subject, and he in turn (the word 'he' shows that we are thinking of 'person' here and not of an abstract cognitive agent) cannot be separated from his 'world' including the subsoil of his experiences and the situation in which he speaks. To speak meaningfully, then, is not merely to operate with symbols, but to have something to say and to say it. The problem which arises here is how, on such a view, expressions are identifiable enough for communication to be possible. Those in the operationalist camp among meaning theorists, of course, do not face this problem, as they explain communication through appeal to rules of operation followed in common by those who use the particular language in question. What the phenomenologist can offer here, it seems to me, is, in lieu of discourse a mode of 'addressal'[16] the condition of whose possibility is a shared world of meanings. What the philosopher does on such a view, is not to batter us down with argument, but to invite us to "look again". The speaker-hearer relationship provides the ground-pattern for something that is familiar in the history of philosophy, a continuing communication where, across centuries maybe, meanings are 'fulfilled', and often in ways very different from the

[14]*Critique of Pure Reason*, B XLIV.
[15]*Ibid.*, B XLIV.
[16]This word (*Anreden*) is used by Martin Buber in his *Urdistanz und Beziehung*. Addressal, for Buber, is also combined with what he calls distancing. Heidelberg, 1951, p. 34 f.

originating germinal ideas which set the communication in motion. As an illustration of this we can take the very diverse ways in which the neo-Kantians developed cues taken from the critical philosophy of Kant. Rather than speak of linguistic facts, a rock-bottom which is supposed to provide an infallible court of appeal, we should be sensitive to the thread of communication which links one thinker with another, in this case (in our attempt to understand how the language of philosophy 'works'), the dialogue situation between the philosopher and himself and between himself and others. This, rather than an attempt to dissect a characteristic mode of 'discourse', is to be our cue in examining the phenomenologist's *experience* of the language of philosophy. That Husserl, for example, was thinking of the *experience* of language as we speak it, is shown in this line: "redendvollziehen wir fortlaufend ein inneres, sich mit Worten verschmelzendes, sie gleichsam beseelendes Meinen."[17] The inner act of meaning 'animating' the words is perhaps rather more intelligible than the idea of its 'mingling' with them. At any rate what is important for Husserl is not linguistic expression as a objective phenomenon, an external structure, but as intended. Applied to the language of philosophy we then have this – Husserl is interested in what the *philosopher* is telling *us*. This telling is a witnessing (a verb used by some of the later phenomenologists rather than by Husserl) instead of a tool-using, for there is no ready-made character about this speaking (and there *is* a ready-made character about a tool). The unreflective *Lebenswelt* which sustains and informs experience is a communicative one. So our reflective utterances have a non-reflective fringe about them which nonetheless does not involve us in solipsism, simply because the entire sphere in which experience takes shape is an inter-subjective one.

This should help us in examining the sort of language Husserl uses. I shall refer mainly to the figurative language used to elucidate the role of the Transcendental Ego in the *Ideas*. The psychology of attention is fully drawn on with its vocabulary of zone, fringe and focus, all de-psychologised in the transcendental manner. Husserl then has to put across how the Transcendental Ego is *involved* in consciousness, not in a form-giving capacity, as in Kant, nor in the substantialist/existential manner of Descartes, but yet in a fashion which he believes to be quite indispensable. He writes: "To the *cogito* itself belongs an immanent 'glancing-towards' the object, a directedness which from another side springs forth from the Ego, which can therefore never be absent."[18] Metaphors connected with vision pile up in the text. The glance of the Ego "goes 'through' every actual cogito, and towards the object". But "this visual ray changes with every cogito, shooting forth afresh with each new one as it comes, and disappearing with it. But the Ego remains self-identical."[19] Paragraph 57 finds Husserl struggling to express what he means by 'pure Ego'

[17]*Formale und transzendentale Logik*, Halle, 1929, p. 20.
[18]*Ideas*, trans. W.R. Boyce Gibson, p. 121.
[19]*Ibid.*, p. 172.

and not finding in abstract philosophical terminology language adequate for his purpose. We have the Cartesian vocabulary of 'cogitatio' and 'cogito', of an element which is self-identical and necessary; we have the Kantian "I think". Negatively, we know that as a result of the suspension of empirical subjectivity something must remain as a residuum. It follows that no *empirical* description will suffice; nor is any kind of inference to transcendent entities in order. How is one to elucidate a non-constituted transcendence, a transcendence in immanence? Bearing Husserl's problems in mind we find that the metaphorical expressions he uses serve him well. The 'associated commonplaces' conjured up include those of a turning towards (implied in glancing); a mobility such that attention can shift quickly from one object to another; the 'through' idea suggests that the ego is thoroughly immersed in experience, coloured by it, and yet, so to say, comes out the other end, so that it is not completely *identified* with any particular experience. The image of rays shooting out from a centre may, to the unsympathetic, suggest a lighthouse model of knowledge. But a closer study of Husserl, especially of the *Krisis*, should correct any such impression. Husserl is not at all in favour of the spectator conception of the knower. But unless experience is *centred* in some way we shall be reduced to a buzzing blooming confusion. It is precisely this centreing that the Transcendental Ego provides. Husserl's thinking often uses the centre/penumbra image. Another associated image is that of a nucleus. In elaborating the structures of consciousness he employs as many transfers of vocabulary as he conveniently can – stratification, dovetailing, horizon etc. along with traditional philosophical terms like morphe, hyle, the doxic and so on. Husserl, in fact, is a very striking case of a philosopher who shows great inventiveness in his use of language, while at the same time he is classical enough in his posing of philosophical issues and often in his adoption of traditional technical terms.

In Husserl's work metaphorical language finds an integral place in the *elucidation* of a standpoint. An approach is built up, a way of looking offered to us as an alternative. In keeping with the German tradition of philosophical scholarship, Husserl is sparing in his use of examples. When an example occurs it is so striking that it attracts comment. Perhaps his chief example in *Ideas* is the reference to the blossoming tree where he is able to pinpoint essences as immanent objects, to distinguish the 'real' and the immanent and make clear how his view differs from phenomenalist perspectivism. There is no particular difficulty in seeing what use Husserl makes of this example.

Husserl is not a philosopher who indulges in florid prose, and this why the inventive character of a great deal of the language he uses should not escape us. To speak of the unity of consciousness as "a flow of phenomena, unlimited at both ends", or of an "immanent 'time' without beginning or end, a time that no chronometers measure"[20] is to speak imaginatively no doubt. In the

---

[20]Vide *Philosophy as Rigorous Science*.

empirical world a flow has a beginning and an end, but there is no difficulty in imagining one that has not. Husserl in using this image cleverly warns us off the associationist fixation on antecedents, on beginnings, and the teleologist's notion of fixed ends. He is not giving us an *argument*. He rather offers an invitation to understand consciousness in a certain way. As for a time that no chronometers measure, the musician is already familiar with the 'virtual' time of musical works, a nexus of unity, and this provides a thoroughly intelligible cue to enable us to grasp the author's meaning, what he 'intends' to say. Many are familiar with the small-change science fictions, Bronson et al., of many writers on self-identity who no doubt exercise considerably imaginative ingenuity in thinking up hypothetical situations which are commonly conceived to provide *arguments* thereby for certain theories, and show them up as convincing. But the conceiving of a hypothetical case which exceeds fantasy provides no argument. However, the stress in our present context is not on this. The linguistic analyst *does* exercise imagination quite often. But he is often too ready to dub as fantasy the linguistic imagination displayed by others, too ready to see in the subtle texture of well-written philosophical prose non-analytic in temper, something not properly philosophical.

Gilbert Ryle's writings tend to betray this attitude in the few cases where he has tilted swords with phenomenologists and existentialists. Reviewing Heidegger's *Sein and Zeit*[21] he says of the technical terms of science and philosophy that "it is at least arguable that it is here, and not in the language of the village and the nursery, that mankind has made a partial escape from metaphor".[22] A little later he introduces the phrase 'dangerous metaphor': "But while it is a dangerous metaphor to speak of acts having 'meanings' or of things as being the 'meanings of acts', it is a fatal error to speak of a thing known as the correlate of a knowing-act as if that implied that we could get to the heart of the thing by analysing our experience of knowing it."[23] Now the adjectives Ryle uses to qualify metaphors bear scrutiny. Here is another: "Why is it not merely a tasteless metaphor, but a flat impropriety, to speak of 'peering at Remorse', 'gazing at Induction', 'taking a long look at Choice', or 'happening to light on Conscience'?"[24] But good marks are awarded elsewhere. Husserl and Wittgenstein used "the illuminating metaphors" of "logical syntax" and "logical grammar".[25] And he himself uses a couple of colourful ones in the same paper, "category-skids" and "logical howlers". In 1951 he granted that our ordinary ways of describing our ponderings and musings tend to be

---

[21]*Mind*, XXXVIII, 1928.

[22]*Ibid*., pagination from *Collected Papers*, Vol. I, p. 206-7.

[23]*Ibid*., p. 212.

[24]Review of Marvin Farber's *The Foundations of Phenomenology* in *Philosophy*, Vol. 21, 1946. *Collected Papers*, p. 220.

[25]"Use, usage and meaning" in *Proceedings of the Aristotelian Society*, Sup. Vol. 35, 1961. *Collected Papers*, Vol. II.

graphic and not literal.[26] But, his own practice shows that graphic language is not only confined to this. So, his precept apart, how does Ryle himself employ metaphor?

It must be recognised that Ryle's metaphors have a natural place in a racy, epigrammatic style peppered with a mordant wit. Illustrations, jokes, snide asides, puns, smoking-room witticisms, all tumble over each other in such a way that the reader can expect a chuckle on almost every page. Perhaps of no other philosopher can the latter be said. Ryle shares the general analytic fixation on things gone wrong. There are puzzles, blocks, and tangles galore. While his colleagues are in cages, traps, fly bottles and assorted claustrophobic situations (cf. Kant's agoraphobic 'empty space'), Ryle is snarled up in various kinds of networks and traffic jams. The kind of jam he is acutely aware of bears a close relation, needless to say, to the sort of things he thinks go wrong in philosophy. There are, historically, plenty of ways of discrediting philosophical theories and arguments. Here is a random sample: picking out fallacies, inconsistencies, unproven conclusions, ambiguities, presuppositions, and detecting the inheriting of other's theoretical lumber. The crowning types of nit-picking for Ryle are, however, spotting mis-categorisations and illicit category conjunctions. But he is very conscious of the delicacy of these tasks. There is something almost Pelagian about them (my phrase). Can't one be almost too self-conscious about philosophising? As he puts it: "The centipede of the poem ran well until he began to wonder how he ran."[27] It is quite an admission for an advocate of what broadly falls under the method of description to say that "the philosopher's description of a concept is bound to terminate in a stammer."[28] But the use of metaphors in Ryle's own 'elucidations' serve him well in making his central argument (it is an argument I think which can be detected in most of his multifarious writings) that the philosopher's business is with conceptual questions and that these are also inter-conceptual ones. What the philosopher primarily does is to shed light by bringing about reallocations. The advocacy of a reallocation is guided by the belief that certain idioms are *appropriate* to a particular category of facts.

Turbayne might find that all the metaphors Ryle uses constitute one vast mixed metaphor. But the individual metaphors are interesting and we shall have to see if they pull or do not pull in different directions. The philosopher's job is said to be "always to investigate the *modi operandi* of all the threads of a spider's web of inter-working concepts...."[29] The same passage also contains the notion of a single concept being out of focus, making "all its associates" also out of focus. There at least two germinal images here, one of intricacy (the spider's web) and the other (really impossible to translate) perhaps that of

---

[26]"Thinking and Language", P.A.S. Sup. Vol. 25, 1951, *Collected Papers*, Vol. II, p. 261.
[27]*Collected Papers*, Vol. I, p. 256.
[28]*Ibid.*, p. 187-8.
[29]*Collected Papers*, Vol. I, p. 189.

excessive or inadequate stress vis-à-vis the rest (of the field of vision). The idea of fixing a concept in its proper position suggests that there is a proper position for it to be in. Here there is a touch of the ring-master's whip about the programme. This impression is supported by a remark in the review of Farber's book to which reference has already been made. We need to *fix* rules of use, and not gaze "at any wearers of labels".[30] The ring-master becomes a traffic-policeman in a paper written in 1954.[31] Philosophical problems arise "as the traffic-policeman's problems arise, when crowds of conceptual vehicles, of different sorts and moving in different directions meet at some conceptual cross-roads...in its early stages, a philosophical dispute is a traffic-block – a traffic-block which cannot be tidied up by the individuals driving their individual cars efficiently." The image is analogous to the spider's web one, but untidier. The supervenient activity of the traffic-policeman (the analyst) is made to seem indispensable. *Dilemmas*, published in the same year, contains further topographical metaphors. A live issue is a "piece of country in which no one knows which way to go".[32] In fact the whole book bristles with figures of speech. There are 'pivot-concepts', concepts which have a "concrete, groundfloor employment", "pieces of theoretical harness" (Where is the horse? The problem? Ordinary language?). The spider's web is there again: "I buzz but I do not get clear."[33] We rummage in 'philosophical thickets'.[34] The new one is the litigation idea – where we have theories purporting to be answers to *different* problems and which yet seem to conflict. Yet here too the core point is the same. What we need is a proper sorting out of concepts, and it is the philosopher's job to do this. There is a rare infelicity – to be in a dilemma is to be 'pinched' (squeezed?) – giving a rather different 'picture' from that of the quandary of Buridan's ass.

The topographical idea is further developed in a paper in 1962.[35] The relation between the philosopher's philosophical and non-philosophical moments is brought out through the analogy of a villager asked to draw or consult a map of his village and who "has, so to speak, to *translate* and therefore to re-think his local topographical knowledge into universal cartographical terms". We have the analogy of two topographical levels. The point of the analogy between analysis and cartography can be briefly mentioned as follows. Examining a concept is examining it in relation to its many neighbour-concepts, just as the cartographer is concerned with the

---

[30] *Ibid.*, p. 221.
[31] "Proofs in Philosophy" (Originally in *Revue internationale de Philosophie*, Vol. 8) *Ibid.*, Vol. II, p. 325.
[32] *Dilemmas*, p. 13.
[33] *Ibid.*, p. 92.
[34] *Ibid.*, p. 111.
[35] "Abstractions", *Dialogue (Canadian Philosophical Review)* Vol. I, *Collected Papers*, Vol. II, p. 441.

relation of a place to other places on the map. Secondly, we already know how to use the concept in the ordinary way just as the villager already knows how to go to place X. Thirdly, in both we have to do with directions and limits.

The map idea is a fairly simple one and familiar enough in the context of Wittgenstein's interest in maps, diagrams and scale-models. But along with it Ryle brings in something else – "implication threads". I quote the passage in full: "When two or twenty familiar implication threads seem to pull across and against one another, it is no longer enough to be able to pull across and against one another, it is no longer enough to be able unperplexedly to follow along each one by itself. We need to be able to state their directions, their limits and their interlockings; to think systematically *about* what normally we merely think competently and even dexterously *with*."[36] The image is a complicated one. We have to "tug" the implication threads that a concept contributes to the statements in which it occurs, and moreover "tug these threads through their neighbouring threads, which, in their turn, he must simultaneously be tugging". At least here we come across a picturesque *verb*. To think systematically *about* is, presumably, to bring into being a second order set of implication threads and even in this latter set there will be what he calls "cross-bearings" The thread idea turns up again when he is discussing J.L. Austin. Austin, he says, would "snatch up the tangled old skein of Determinism, Freedom and Responsibility or of Knowledge, Self-Knowledge and Belief; or of Sense-Perception, Appearance and Reality; and unceremoniously shake it inside out.

"These brusquely inverted skeins had their own knots, twists and loose ends, but not the inveterate, obstinate ones. Fingers severely drilled in piecemeal unravelling might actually undo these fresh, unaggravated tangles. But it was the impatient shake that made the difference."[37]

The thing is to get things straight. One is, I suppose, not to take the metaphor too far. To say that wool is made up into balls, used for knitting etc. would be to go beyond what was intended. We are supposed to set getting things straight alongside getting concepts 'correctly' allocated, mapped etc. Ryle himself grants the usefulness of using *different* analogies and plays upon words when he writes:[38] "The harm done by subjugation to one picture is partly repaired by deliberately ringing the changes on two or three. If they are appropriate at all, they are likely to be appropriate in different ways and therefore to keep us reminded of features which otherwise we might forget." These features concern "conceptual facts". A similar point was made by John Wisdom: "...in accepting *all* the systems their blinding power is broken, their revealing power becomes acceptable; the individual is restored to us, not isolated as before we used language, not, in a box as when language mastered

[36] *Ibid.*, p. 444.
[37] Review of "Symposium on J.L. Austin", *Listener*, 1970, vide *Collected Papers*, Vol. I., p. 274.
[38] "Pleasure", P.A.S. Sup. Vol. 27, 1954, *Collected Papers*, Vol. II, p. 334.

us, but in 'creation's chorus'."[39] One final example, Ryle's own metaphor for Wittgenstein's method, "the tea-tasting method",[40] might well be applied to his own technique: Tea-tasters "savour each sample and try to place it next door to its closest neighbours, and this not in respect of just one discriminable quality but along the lengths of various lines of quality". This certainly recommends a sort of classification. But we have moved a long way from the logician's "perforated screens", "stencil slots" and "litmus-paper". So all in all what Ryle does 'ambulando' in his philosophising, although radically different from what Heidegger does "am Weg", makes adventurous use of the resources of language in presenting both overall points of view and specific strategies of argument.

The *Concept of Mind* has been sufficiently discussed and this not the place to take up the cudgels on behalf of the Cartesian 'myth'. A few questions, however, can be posed in conclusion. What to X is a category preference appears as a 'myth' to Y. But what is a myth? In the *Concept of Mind*, we hear, "A myth is, of course, not a fairy story. It is the presentation of facts belonging to one category in the idioms appropriate to another."[41] But who is to decide what idiom is appropriate to what category? The 'one world' idiom of the *Concept of Mind* may seem to the phenomenologist very inappropriate to all those 'meanings', immanent contents of subjective life, which he finds to be the proper topic of description. Once we admit alternative pictures, as Ryle does in his recommending of 'ringing the changes', our whole notion of what is 'appropriate' undergoes a radical transformation. In this respect some of Ryle's own metaphors are "dangerous" vis-a-vis his own philosophical position. Some "systematic restatements" and reallocations may make things worse, that is, in analytic perspective, they may work against the elucidation of discourse. They may lead, for example, to those neither fish nor fowl peculiarities, "mongrel-categoricals". The threads of implication of Ryle's own metaphors are indeed very involved. Sometimes they need to be tugged, and sometimes left as they are, because if language gets tied up in knots it is because, glory be, we just cannot "fix rules of use" in an ex cathedra manner, and certainly not through appeal to ordinary language.

---

[39]"Philosophy, Anxiety and Novelty", *Mind* Vol. LXIII, 1944. reprinted in *Philosophy and Psycho-Analysis*, p. 119.

[40]Article on Ludwig Wittgenstein, In *Analysis*, Vol. XII, 1951, *Collected Papers*, Vol. I, p. 225.

[41]*The Concept of Mind*, p. 8.

CHAPTER VI

Subversion and Intention

From the question of choices of metaphor and category preference in general it is but a hop, skip and a jump to the question of what determines them, and thereby springs into view one of the bogeys that haunt the contemporary philosopher, that of subterranean influence, the iceberg under the water – the whole Freudian mythology of upstairs and downstairs and the skeletons in the murky basement. The price paid for abandoning faculty psychology, for rummaging in the pedigree of thought, some say, is a thorough-going debunking of all pretensions to true statement, correct theorising, and valid reasoning. The things that philosophers say, on this view, have about as much credibility as the Emperor's new clothes. And yet attempts to subvert, whether in politics or elsewhere, are often in the long run unsuccessful, threatening though they may seem when they first rear their heads. So all this merits looking into before alarm and despondency take their toll.

Although Freud, or rather those who claim to be influenced by him, is the main figure behind twentieth-century psychologistic debunkers, there are precedents which need to be mentioned first. Fichte wrote: "The kind of philosophy a man chooses depends upon the kind of man he is. For a philosophic system is no piece of dead furniture one can acquire and discard at will. It is animated with the spirit of the man who possesses it."[1] This linking of types of philosophy with types of temperament does not have the subversive potential that the following passage from Nietzsche's *Beyond Good and Evil* has: "As little as the act of birth comes into consideration in the whole process and procedure of heredity, just as little is 'being conscious', *opposed* to the instinctive in any decisive sense, the greater part of the conscious thinking of a philosopher is secretly influenced by his instincts and forced into definite channels." Alexander Herzberg authored a book called *The Psychology of Philosophers* and William James wrote that "the history of philosophy is to a great extent that of a certain clash of human temperaments."[2] James Harvey Robinson is even more specific:[3] "A history of philosophy and theology could

---

[1] *First Introduction to the Science of Knowledge*, Sämtliche Werke I, 434.
[2] *Pragmatism*, p. 6.
[3] *The Mind in the Making*, 1921, p. 45.

be written in terms of grouches, wounded pride, and aversions, and it would be far more instructing than the usual treatment of these themes."

Freud's work originally appeared in a clinical context, but was soon found to have far-reaching implications in respect of his unmasking of the disguise of thought, his probing into its credentials. If all "psychical productions" belong to the area of meaning, language is not a unique lens through which reality is to be spied, but takes its place amidst dreams, symbolic gestures and actions, in fact a whole range of phenomena which can be regarded as symbolic. The distinction between latent and manifest content burst on a philosophical public already familiar with the distinction between the noumenal and the phenomenal. But the Freudian 'latent' content, so far from being noumenal, had to do with what Hume called the "sensitive" part of our nature, and in far more explosive a manner than Hume could dream of. But we are back on Humean territory in the sense that in lieu of abstract generalities we now had habits which had been christened 'forces', a new dynamism of the psyche where pure reason received a far bigger dressing down than any given by Kant. The unconscious was conceived by Freud as a reservoir of *power,* and it was this non-rational power which pulled the strings. The prime factor at work, above all, was *desire*. Unconscious desires lead us to weave a web of illusions which enable us "to bear the burden of existence". In this way the unconscious dispossesses the conscious mind as the spearhead of meaning. The implications are serious for "rational thought", for if the unconscious is the origin of meaning, then arguments, theories and all the rest, are not actually *in our control.* This amounts to saying that the constructs of conscious thought are hardly distinguishable from "dream-work". The 'Id' sounds in all this suspiciously like Plato's 'tyrant', a centre of 'dynamis' or power. If reasoning is nothing other than rationalization, 'universality', 'objectivity', the distinction between true and false, all seem to have been abolished at one go.

The Freudian analysis, like the Marxist, claimed to be an analysis of what was "actually going on behind the scenes". The therapy recommended by each, however, was very different. Whereas Freud thought that by bringing to light our complexes we would be able, essentially, to adjust ourselves to the status quo (what else after all could his upper middle class Viennese patients be expected to do), the Marxist unmasking reckoned to provide cues for *altering* the status quo, that is for altering the institutional framework of society in keeping with the changes taking place among the various forces of production. In philosophy and literature things were not "left as they were" after Freud produced his bombshell. The philosopher's traditional function as discriminator between truth and falsity seemed to have been radically undermined. Literary critics were divided into those who saw an inevitably debunking potential in reliance on biographical data and those who saw in it a legitimate aid to assessment of literary works of art. There was something rather similar in the nature of the blow that both literary critics and philosophers received. Literary criticism had taken pains in weaning itself from romanticism (which had put all talk of 'origins' on a pedestal), and philosophers, not all no doubt, had been carefully weaning themselves from naturalistic fallacies. The recoil from Freud was parallel in both cases. Literary critics (some of them rather) took refuge in structuralism, in concentration on the nature of the work of art, the text itself; and linguistic analysts consoled themselves with linguistic games per se. The rumbles subsided. Or did they?

When H.H. Price said in 1951[4] that "the really important work of thinking is very often done below the threshold of consciousness" he did not have any very sinister processes in mind. Price did not take the line that the philosopher's pronouncements, in consequence, appear in a sort of disguise. We need rather to look at the work of J.O. Wisdom, John Wisdom and Morris Lazerowitz to feel the measure of the impact that psycho-analysis has had on twentieth-century philosophy. John Oulton Wisdom's study of Berkeley[5] shows the direct influence of Freud, rather than, as in John Wisdom's case, the influence of Freud via Wittgenstein. He tries to find out the links between the development of philosophical ideas, modifications of temperament, organic changes and philosophical climate. Wisdom's analysis of Berkeley's work is weighted on the side of physiological factors which he takes as determining conditions. Like Turbayne, he is concerned to 'unmask', but Wisdom's mode of unmasking has more of a debunking outcome then does that of Turbayne, for whereas the latter seems to tell us, "As long as we know what's going on, it's all right", Wisdom's moral is more radical. What is of relevance to this discussion is Wisdom's own assessment of what searching out the unconscious origin of Schopenhauer's or Descartes' or Berkeley's philosophy may be supposed to do for us. He states the alleged gains in a very explicit manner. Subterranean discoveries can be regarded as providing a new angle for approaching problems hitherto believed to be intellectual in toto. Furthermore, when we find a particular system depicts a fantasy, this weans us away from questions of truth and falsity which then appear as out of court. But to identify systems as belonging to the realm of fantasy is not to dub them as nonsensical. They do have a *meaning* but it is the sort of meaning which is uncovered by psycho-analysis. This, however, can help us to discover whether there is anything "objective" present or not. Apart from misgivings about a genetic fallacy involved in talk about 'origins' one cannot help wondering why Berkeley's digestive problems or his views on tar-water should be any more relevant to his philosophy than Pythagoras' odd ideas about beans were to his. One way out is to say that the sort of data presented by Wisdom tells us something about *Berkeley* but not about his philosophy. To say this is of course to make a distinction unacceptable to some. Why, it may be objected, should we admit

---

[4] Symposium on "Thinking and Language" in P.A.S. Sup. Vol. XXV, 1951.
[5] *The Unconscious Origin of Berkeley's Philosophy*, London, 1953.

the relevance of biographical details in the interpretation of literary works but deem them irrelevant in considering philosophical writings? One reason for discounting "personal data" goes something like this. Many people are known to have the particular digestive problems, complexes, physiological disabilities that philosophers X, Y and Z are known to have had, but this did not result in their propounding the philosophies that philosophers X, Y and Z propounded. Not all men with club feet turned into a Byron or a Kaiser Wilhelm, and not all poachers write great plays. Not all backgammon players were mitigated sceptics.

The thesis about 'unconscious control' of conscious processes has not always been made from a Freudian base. In Jung's scheme of thinking, for example, appeal is made to the collective unconscious. The Sapir-Whorf hypothesis about language maintains that "the phenomena of a language are to its own speakers largely of a background character, and so are outside the critical consciousness and control of the speaker."[6] Part of this background character includes non-linguistic factors such as the experiences and needs of the speech-community, and the nature and demands of the environment. The critics of the hypothesis have taken it to involve linguistic relativism and this in turn has come under fire for a variety of reasons (e.g. the claim that it makes communication, translation etc. impossible) which do not concern us here. What I mean is that those who talk of backgrounds are not *necessarily* talking of 'unconscious' factors. Backgrounds can be contextual or even dispositional. In his *Notebooks 1914-16*[7] Wittgenstein comments: "Behind our thoughts, true or false, there is always to be found a dark background, which we are only later able to bring into the light and express as a thought." There is no suggestion in this remark that for a thought to have a dark background disqualifies it (or, presumably, the statements which describe it) from being considered true or false. This takes us into matters of Wittgenstein interpretation where the only guides are the scanty hints given by Wittgenstein himself and the opinions of those close to him. After his return to Cambridge in 1929 the material now available in *The Blue and Brown Books* was dictated. No Viennese could fail to be impressed with Freud's path-breaking investigations of the psyche. But the whole apparatus of Super-Ego, Ego and Id was, after all, a theoretical structure intended to throw light on the data, and could be said to constitute a mythology of its own. The therapeutic language Wittgenstein himself uses lends some support to the view that he, somehow or other, became the psychoanalyst of philosophy, uncovering things that had been hidden, dissolving problems, demystifying them and so on. This view is lent support by quotations like: the "treatment of a philosophical question is like the treatment of an

---

[6] Benjamin Lee Whorf, *Thought, Language and Reality*, 1959, p. 211.
[7] 36e.

illness",[8] and "the sickness of philosophical problems can get cured only through a changed mode of thought and of life".[9]

But there is much to puzzle us in all this. In *The Blue Book*[10] we are told that "philosophy, as we use the word, is a fight against the fascination which forms of expression exert upon us". Alice Ambrose elaborates this by saying that central to Wittgenstein's understanding of the philosopher's activity is that "in arguing for a 'view' a philosopher evidences a dissatisfaction with ordinary language".[11] Illuminating as this is, there are two things that bother me about it. First of all, Wittgenstein insists that ordinary language is all right. In the *Yellow Book* he is reported to say "what the bedmaker says is all right, but what the philosophers say is all wrong". Is it what the philosopher *says about* ordinary language that is wrong, or the way he himself uses it that is wrong? The second difficulty is that to have something new to say is not to be *dissatisfied* with current usage, but (in Wittgenstein's own idiom) to play a *new* language game. We need to get back to the analogy with psycho-analysis. The main thrust of the analogy seems to be the stress on 'unmasking', on things not being as they appear (the distinction between real and apparent is, as we all know, a very hoary one in the history of philosophy). But there is something else in Freud's analysis which pulls in a rather different and tantalising direction. Freud's clinical experience led him to the discovery of psycho-analysis as a method of dealing with pathological phenomena. The 'dealing with' can be unpacked into *understanding* their meaning, an understanding which, when it dawns in the patient, amounts to a cure. But to discover the same processes at work in dreams and the "psychopathology of everyday life" is actually to remove the theoretical demarcation between the abnormal and the normal (the practical demarcation in terms of behaviour, seriousness of symptoms, 'orientation', self-direction etc. of course remains). Some of Freud's patients made intriguing slips of the tongue which he refers to in his *Psychopathology of Everyday Life*. The 'meaning' of these slips is analysed in detail by Freud. But, as we noticed earlier, to play upon words was a very familiar phenomenon in sophisticated Viennese conversation. We have, then, a kind of continuum of verbal play where underground meanings can be both detected and (in the case of puns) enjoyed. While one way of looking at this is to say how close the neurotic is to everyday life, another viewpoint sees the double-meaning, the symbolic, as part and parcel of the everyday.

Now in his *Philosophical Investigations*,[12] Wittgenstein speaks of "normal language games". Presumably these are those that relate to reality. So the

---

[8]*Philosophical Investigations*, p. 91.
[9]*Remarks on the Foundations of Mathematics*, p. 57.
[10]p. 27.
[11]"The Yellow Book Notes in relation to the Blue Book", *Critica*, Vol. IX, No. 26, Mexico, August 1977.
[12]142.

criterion of normality for both Freud and Wittgenstein seems to be the reality principle. But is there in fact a break between the sanctified normal language games of the market-place (those of the bedmaker) and the other kind where we are bewitched, fascinated etc. by certain forms of expression? That Wittgenstein speaks of two kinds of philosophizing is common knowledge, the kind to be eschewed and the kind to be espoused. The former is the kind that succumbs to certain forms of expression (the dictates of grammar being even higher up on the list of undesirables than misleading analogies etc.) and the latter being the kind that is "a fight against the fascination which forms of expression exert upon us".[13] But the fight can after all only be carried on by using other forms of expression. The language that philosophers use is of the same currency as the language they use in non philosophical moments. It was this inherently Pelagian (my expression) character of the philosopher's task that at times reduced Wittgenstein, I truly believe, to despair. The whispered dictate "Physician, heal thyself" haunts the philosophical consciousness. The peculiarity of what the philosopher is doing, the non-sacrosanct character of the language he uses, adds a certain poignancy to his task. It is common knowledge that psycho-analysts undergo psycho-analysis themselves. The continuity that there is between our philosophical and non-philosophical uses of language is hinted at by Wittgenstein only in his language-game metaphor. We have already discussed this metaphor earlier. Here it is necessary to add that in the present context the metaphor does not serve him well. The game metaphor suggests the autonomy of language, for games have no point beyond themselves. They require no justification. But the main thing about what he calls "normal" language games is that they relate to reality in contradistinction to occasions when language idles, is on holiday etc.

For both Freud and Wittgenstein it is convention that is bedrock. When we wake up, the dream world comes to an end. It is not possible concurrently to function in the dream world and in the real world. The patient is cured when he leaves his fantasies and adjusts to Alfred Doolittle's world of middle class morality (to switch from Vienna to London). But those who undertake the verbal style of cure often relapse again, and, in these post-Freudian days, are advised to go in for chemotherapy, or even shock treatment. As far as concurrent functioning is concerned, this is precisely the problem with the philosopher. He has both philosophical and non-philosophical moments. The solipsist writes letters to his friends, the sceptic sits on chairs without testing them first, and the Absolutist is confident that 2 + 2 make 4 absolutely when settling with the grocer. This is where the analogy between psycho-analysis and philosophy seems to split apart at the seams. Freud's system turns on his distinction between the pleasure principle and the reality principle. But the sceptic is most worried about his scepticism and the solipsist about his

---

[13] *The Blue Book*, p. 27.

solipsism, and certainly Wittgenstein never ceased to agonize over the implications of his own view of language, for it meant in fact that there *could* be no cure, we would always be caught up in some language game or other. No doubt there can be a language game in which the purpose of words is to call up images, and the game played between psycho-analyst and patient is perhaps something like this. In such cases "uttering a word is like striking a note on the keyboard of the imagination".[14] And some keyboards jangle in a nightmare fashion. The crunch is that one man's illusion is another man's reality. The Marxist will say that nothing is more illusory than the cushioned comfort of the middle class everyday world. There is a hollowness about the victory which replaces the fantastic by the commonplace, the strictures of one fly bottle by the jammy confines of yet another.

John Wisdom's work drews on both Freud and Wittgenstein and perhaps this combination of influences gives his approach a somewhat elusive character. Wisdom is no less a stylist than Ryle. But his characteristic uses of metaphors, epigrams, illustrations and jokes do not serve to carry an argument forward to the extent we found to obtain in the case of Ryle's philosophising. Primeval oceans churn, lighthouses occasionally beam, but we are not conspicuously forrader. In 1933 he made a pronouncement which caught philosophical attention at the time: "...the philosophic stimulus is not a request for information, but a request for insight."[15] Three years[16] later he spoke of the philosopher's intention as being this: "to bring out relations between categories of being, between spheres of language...." A clinical metaphor also makes its appearance. Philosophical theories are spoken of as "symptoms" of linguistic penetration. His paper on "Philosophy and Psycho-analysis" in 1946[17] continues the clinical theme. Philosophical doubt and obsessional doubt are compared and an analogy is drawn between philosophical and other sorts of stress. Both philosophers and patients go in for justificatory talk. The paradoxical character of philosophical theories is brought out. To say "Matter exists" or "Matter does not exist" is, in each case, to speak paradoxically. Such statements, he thinks. come from extraordinary experience, and "extraordinary experience of the ordinary called for extraordinary use of ordinary language".[18] A paradox is "not established by experiment", and yet "declares...a discovery in the familiar".[19] At the close of this paper Wisdom underlines the comparisons between philosophical reasoning and psycho-analytical procedure. Philosophical discussion brings out latent opposing forces. What is unearthed includes not only latent linguistic sources but non-linguistic sources (this was

---

[14]*Philosophical Investigations*, No. 6.
[15]"Ostentation", *Psyche*, Vol. XIII. Reprinted in *Philosophy and Psycho-analysis*, 1953, p. 12.
[16]"Philosophical Perplexity", PAS., Vol. XVI, As above, p. 39.
[17]*Polemic* No. 4.
[18]*Ibid.*, *Philosophy and Psycho-analysis*, p. 177.
[19]*Ibid.*, p. 178.

quite a new thing for a practitioner of the linguistic analytic method to say). For this reason a purely linguistic treatment of philosophical conflicts is often inadequate, (metaphysical concepts and theories reverberate with "echoes from the heart"). The non-linguistic sources of philosophical thinking are precisely those that trouble us elsewhere in our lives. Wisdom comes very near to comparing a philosophical paradox with a complex in so far as a complex is an emotionally tinged idea, something subterranean which exerts power, occasions conflicts and cannot be got at save through the application of relevant technique. But he does not, at least in this paper, mention this comparison in so many words. In fact he stresses that "philosophy has never been merely a psychogenic disorder nor is the new philosophical technique merely a therapy".[20] The difference is that "philosophers reason for and against their doctrines and in doing so show us not new things but old things anew".[21] No doubt this is an echo of the dictum that philosophy leaves everything as it is. Similarly the psycho-analyst helps the patient to adjust. "Knowing" enables one to accept situations for what they are. If philosophy is not informative then one cannot claim to know new things through philosophising. The psycho-analyst doesn't make new people of us, but helps us to accept ourselves as we are.

The penetrative power that some philosophical theories evince is discussed in further detail in "Philosophy, Metaphysics and Psycho-analysis".[22] The sceptic penetrates a disguise which no one usually penetrates (so also does the novelist, Wisdom recognises). Perhaps the sceptic's and the solipsist's positions are queerest, the most analogous to pathological states. Metaphysicians are said to "bring into the light certain old established and invaluable models...."[23] Some of them illuminate and some distort. But all are *unconscious*. To bring them to light is to make them conscious, and this in turn means "we may control them instead of their controlling us, so that we may see how they illuminate and how they distort". Some models are found to be "inappropriate" (e.g. deductive ones). So we have a new variation on the *Phaedrus* charioteer model, with the linguistic analyst whipping the unruly horses which now function in the light of day instead of in the subterranean kingdom of the shades.

Now, how far can these metaphors of unmasking, penetrating disguises and recognising the familiar take us? Wisdom's most important insight, it can be said, is his recognition of a non-linguistic component which is other than brute fact. In this respect his position resembles the Wittgenstein of the middle and last periods rather than the Wittgenstein of the *Tractatus*. But if the non-linguistic component includes not only contextual and situational factors to do with forms of life but the imponderables within man himself, and here he is

[20]*Ibid.*, p. 181.
[21]*Ibid.*, p. 181.
[22]Vide *Philosophy and Psycho-analysis*, pp. 248-82.
[23]*Ibid.*, p. 274.

surely at his most insightful, how is a philosopher to exercise the element of "control" which is being advocated? Then is he not perhaps laying too much stress on recognition of the *familiar*? What is familiar was not always such. We begin with the unfamiliar and it gradually becomes familiar. We often stretch the familiar over the unfamiliar in an attempt to make it familiar, until we learn to accept the unfamiliar on its own terms. For example, the man familiar with classical music automatically starts listening for resolutions when he comes across atonal music for the first time. Later he learns to listen in a different way, and accept the new for its own sake (he may react violently of course!).

The crunch comes next. If all our model-making, categorial frameworks, linguistic innovations and the rest hinge on imponderables within man himself, does this or does this not reduce all our endeavours in model-making etc. to the status of *illusion*? No one has been as outspoken about this as Morris Lazerowitz, and his views expressed in a series of important books have not received the serious attention they deserve. It is Lazerowitz who, most of all, links the pedigree of thought with the credentials of thought in a way which is, or should be, highly disturbing to the philosopher, and in a way which could not be anticipated by Kant when he spoke of transcendental illusion. For Kant, the dialectic of illusion is triggered when categories are misemployed under the regulative guidance of those principles which tempt us to tear down all boundaries, all categorial demarcations. But what if those very demarcations are purely contingent? Kant is protected from any such view by his own methodological demarcation between the empirical and the transcendental. Husserl is likewise protected against it by his distinction between the naturalistic and the phenomenological levels of analysis. But what if we start with the natural man, warts and all, imponderables and all? Lazerowitz, taking cues both from Freud and Wittgenstein starts just here.

Beginning with *The Structure of Metaphysics,* published in 1955, Lazerowitz has been progressively engaged in a task of "semantic unmasking", where we are shown that the philosopher's claims to make true statements are in fact spurious claims. We have already noticed how the appearance/reality dichotomy of the ontologists is substituted by analysts with dichotomies like "what you think you are doing when you philosophize and what you are actually doing", and "what you think you are saying and what you are actually saying" The metaphor of therapy, for some, threw light on the peculiar position that philosophers were believed to be in. But there were doubts whether the patient could ever be cured and disagreements as to what perfect health would be like. Even so, diagnostic talk has had a long run for its money. Lazerowitz's three-tiered analysis of philosophical theories owes a lot to Freud and Wittgenstein but is no mere amalgam of their ideas.

In *Studies in Metaphilosophy* (1964), which in many ways gives the clearest statement of his position, he rings the changes on an oft-quoted metaphor of

Bradley by saying that "the practice of philosophy generally may well be described as a ballet of linguistic moves and counter-moves". It has certainly tended to be so in recent decades, with Wittgenstein cast as the shadow choreographer. The terminological alterations that philosophers introduce, he says,[24] "cannot be shown wrong by recourse to examination of usage, and the resistance to such an alteration cannot be shown correct by recourse to usage" How then are we to look on them? They reflect "fantasy-satisfying revision of usage...or a resistance to a revision".[25] Philosophical theories "have made deep connection with unconscious material in our mind".[26] What this deep connection may be is left for the time being unclarified. To have a deep connection with is not necessarily to be caused by, or to spring from. The metaphysician is said to play a game with language and the revised language is a "dummy language" which has fantasy value. The illusion spun by the metaphysician is made up of dummy language plus arguments and surrounding talk. This certainly sounds a rather plausible analysis of a supposedly *non*-metaphysical piece of philosophising, the language of sense data.

But there is more to come. The purpose of the new terminology "must be the intellectual deception it perpetuates, an illusion which must connect with deeper material in our minds".[27] The plot thickens here because it is assumed that the linguistic revision must have a rationale behind it. Illusions and delusions are not the result of deliberate strategy. Also the effect produced by the revision "need not" be the effect intended. Perhaps at this point there is an implied contrast between conscious and unconscious intention, something which fits in with Freud's method of analysis. Freud also allows a shadow region which is a mixture of the two. The nature of pathological states is sometimes partly manifest to the patient and partly hidden.

The language of day-dreaming now comes in. The metaphysician is "someone who knows how to day-dream with language, although he is not aware of the nature of what he indulges himself in". The reference to day-dreaming is intended by Lazerowitz to reinforce his point that spinning philosophical theories is like spinning fantasies. Often one spins fantasies knowing fully well that one is doing so. The philosopher, however, is not like this. His "dummy language" creates a delusive idea that something is being said about "a kind of phenomenon". The backdrop of ordinary speech gives the dummy language a certain plausibility, and the metaphysician is rendered capable of "communicating his day-dream to other intellectuals".[28] A metaphysical day-dream "actually expresses thoughts which are unconsciously

[24] p. 67.
[25] *Ibid.*
[26] *Ibid.*, p. 121.
[27] *Ibid.*, p. 161.
[28] *Ibid.*, p. 162.

grasped".[29] So, although the word game which the metaphysician plays makes him and others dupes, "the game answers to needs at many levels of his mind".[30] Wherein lies the duping? We are deceived "that a theory fortified by powerful evidence is being announced".[31] Adapting one of Freud's metaphors, he goes on to say that a philosophical theory "is a structure with one leg in the adult part of our mind, the educated intellect and another leg in the archaic part of our mind, the unconscious".[32] So a philosophical theory is not *quite* on all fours with a day-dream although it resembles it in respect of being a fantasy-making structure. Incidentally, of course, adults do day-dream, and people are not taken in by their day-dreams. One can free-wheel along in imagination in the course of the day-dream, know that one is doing so, consciously prolong it and so on. Lazerowitz is not affected by this would-be hole-picking in the metaphor, for the philosopher too is carrying on a parallel kind of double-think, maintaining fantastic positions in the face of the facts and unmoved by the consideration that 'reality' is otherwise. The three-layer structure of Lazerowitz's analysis is now in the open: "A philosophical theory consists, for one thing, of the statement of an unheralded, concealed alteration of terminology (the sentence we naturally take to be the expression of the theory), for another thing, of the delusive appearance presented to our conscious awareness that the words state a deep theory about the existence or nature of reality, and lastly, of an unconscious fantasy or cluster of fantasies of importance to our emotional welfare."[33] The relevance of psycho-analysis to philosophy is not that we therein find an *analogy* for the unmasking which the analytic philosopher engages in, but psycho-analysis "alone can discover for us what they (the philosophers) really say, as against what they delusively appear to say".[34] This is to maintain that the latent content of philosophical utterances is not philosophical at all. This is the 'hard saying' which emerges out of the proceeding sequence of positions (I am not at all sure that it constitutes an *argument*).

Next it is necessary to see wherein the 'illusions' of philosophers are said to lie. In *Philosophy and Illusion* (1968) it is put thus: The illusion of philosophy is that philosophical utterances have truth-values. What is the 'reality' with which the 'illusion' is contrasted? In brief – linguistic structure plus unconscious purport. The Freudian inspiration of all this naturally leads him to say next that philosophers *like* their fly bottles. We can supposedly read off (or a psycho-analyst could) a philosopher's psychic needs, fears, wishes and obsessions by rooting behind his metaphors, finding out the dark and murky

[29]*Ibid.*, p. 163.
[30]*Ibid.*, p. 174.
[31]*Ibid.*, p. 179.
[32]*Ibid.*, p. 180.
[33]*Ibid.*, p. 217.
[34]*Ibid.*, p. 256.

story behind his language preferences. The thesis by now uncannily resembles at one extreme the sort of thing Marxists say about the unseen working of forces in society, and at the other, the appeal to "real will" made by a certain kind of idealist political philosopher at the turn of the century. But if things are *never* as they appear to be, are we ever in a position to say, of a particular case, "This is not what it appears to be"? Even Wittgenstein grants that *some* of the philosopher's propositions are true, e.g. "It is an hypothesis that the sun will rise tomorrow: and this means that we do not *know* whether it will rise."[35] To return to Lazerowitz; What the philosopher *does* do (in lieu of the pursuit of truth) is to draw new linguistic boundaries.[36] This is not to announce a claim to a discovery which could be exposed as true or false (genuine or spurious?) but to make a recommendation, a recommendation, moreover, which has unconscious prompting. But even if we accept this analysis and set about the detective work of unearthing the unconscious factors, how are we to distinguish between the "colourful gibes which need not be taken seriously"[37] (and among which the reference to language going on holiday is to be included) and matters of more pith and moment? Is the phrase "family resemblance", which seems chock-a-block with teasing possibilities, to slip through the analytic net or should we burrow away at it? Does it qualify, one might ask somewhat irreverently, for the label "gerry-mandered piece of terminology",[38] which is Lazerowitz's latest nomenclature for the metaphysician's linguistic innovations?

The problem is that *some* linguistic strategies seem to slip by. When we remap language, so as to bring to light hidden contradictions or show up paradoxes, we earn a pat on the back. But Lazerowitz is very frank and honest about the achievements of the 'good guys': "...analysis as a technique of investigation in other parts of philosophy (other than perception) has been no more successful in obtaining solid, uncontested results than have the techniques used in metaphysics."[39] What seems to work most against the philosopher's laudable attempt to enlarge his understanding, on Lazerowitz's view, is not so much the unconscious pedigree of thought as the *belief* that "exotic language preferences" have revelatory power, that they enable us to say something new about the cosmos. He puts it like this: "A belief that derives its strength from a wish rather than from evidence is an illusion."[40] The point is really even more far-reaching. If the Freudian part of what Lazerowitz says is taken seriously, he should have said "unconscious wish" rather than just

---

[35]*Philosophical Investigations*, 6.36311.
[36]*Ludwig Wittgenstein, Philosophy and Language*, Morris Lazerowitz and Alice Ambrose (ed.), 1972.
[37]*Ibid.*, p. 233.
[38]*The Language of Philosophy*, 1977, p. 174.
[39]*Studies in Metaphilosophy*, p. 159.
[40]*The Language of Philosophy*, p. 163.

"wish". It is difficult to verify the extent to which wishes, unconscious or otherwise, enter into the formulation of philosophical theories. Philosophers seem, more than anything, to agonise over their conclusions. Those who have discussed 'paradoxes' have hardly experienced pleasure over the inconclusive nature of what they had to say. We have no evidence for thinking that the limiting of understanding to a categorial straight-jacket, cavorting on the windy plains of the Absolute, setting up the dummy language of sense data – three very different kinds of philosophical adventure – were all accompanied by feelings of great joy on the part of those who went in for this sort of thing or that any kind of unconscious steam was worked off thereby. In fact no *evidence* one way or the other is in principle available on the issue.

Lazerowitz's findings startle because he has reminded us of a matter of supreme importance which has in recent decades, in fact, ever since "the linguistic turn" made its appearance, been systematically brushed under the carpet. In recognising that philosophical theories are intellectual constructions we need to realise that they are none the less at the same time psychical productions. This only occasions surprise in a philosophical climate of opinion where philosophers have been desperately trying to have their efforts accomodated under the sheltering umbrella of the *Naturwissenschaften*. Once philosophy is seen to have its rightful place among the *Geisteswissenschaften* much of what Lazerowitz has been reminding us occasions far less alarm and despondency. Since Freud, we have learnt to admit that it is possible to say other than what one means. But it is an entirely different kettle of fish to look on style as inherently a matter of dissimulation, or to regard theoretical constructs as illusory nets cast over the big fish, the whale of all whales – reality.

No doubt there is something quasi-pathological expressed in the blocks, cramps, worries et al. of the analytical philosopher. To substitute Platonic error or opinion by illusion is still to assume, by implication, the possibility of a clear 'daylight' view. Perhaps John Wisdom and Morris Lazerowitz both believe that this is in fact *not* possible. One problem dissolves and another rears its head. The task of unmasking, tinkering, call it what you will, goes on. But instead of looking on knots, enigmas and paradoxes as blocks (ultimates where we have to stop) the 'healthy' philosopher can surely look on them as *provocations*. In other words, instead of assuming, "There must be something wrong", an attitude which it seems to me starts with Russell and goes right through almost all analytic philosophising, one can take the line, "There must be something more here", and go on to see what it is. Knots, problems etc. set thinking in motion rather than bring it to a halt. This is the big difference between the dynamism of thought and the stopping short of physical motion which *is* brought to a halt by barriers, blocks etc. To be reminded of the iceberg beneath the surface, as Freud reminds us, is to remind us that all perspectives are from the 'inside'. The perspective sub specie aeternitatis is not for us. But does an increased understanding of the whence of thought, such as psycho-analysis gives us, subvert irrevocably the 'whither' that on-going thought is found to evince? I do not myself believe that it does. But before we go further we may do worse than to see how literary criticism has reached to the threat of icebergs in wintry seas and leviathans of the deep. For hackles were raised there first, and in fact philosophers have reacted much more tardily to all this than the literary critics did.

When Wimsatt and Beardsley spoke of "the intentional fallacy" in their well-known paper which appeared in 1946[41] they did so on the ground that a certain kind of criticism, the one that relied on digging up biographical data, resulted in the loss of "the work as a linguistic fact".[42] They seemed to conflate biographical data with intention. There was a reason for this, namely, their taking of critical work on Coleridge as one of their chief examples. They granted that there is an "explanatory stratum" (something which philosophers rarely recognise), but in their zeal for structure, they failed to show how this is related to our response to the text. A text (let us use this word so that we can include both literary work and philosophical writing) is said to exist independently of the author and his intention. But the term intention is not a simple one. There can be conscious and unconscious intention (Lazerowitz drew our attention to unconscious intention), declared and undeclared intention (undeclared intention can be conscious), original and subsequent or modified intention, and intention which is worked out along the way. Nor does this exhaust the possibilities. How does this apply to philosophical texts?

It could be said that it was Aristotle's intention to 'answer' various questions raised by Plato, to formulate what he thought to be a metaphysical system which was an improvement on that of Plato. But although philosophers often begin by defining their position in relation to that of others this does not exhaust the content of their intention. When Hume wrote the *Enquiry* he tried to modify what he wrote in the *Treatise* since the latter fell stillborn from the press and failed to make the impact he had anticipated. There was a conscious intention to make the work more concise, for one thing. The section on liberty and necessity was introduced deliberately with a view to making his critique of extant views of the causal relation more complete.

The experimental way in which some works of art originate (for example, some of Rabindranath Tagore's paintings began with doodles, and some free verse develops from associations around a particular word or image) is probably not paralleled in the writing of philosophical texts. But the way in which a metaphor, example, or hypothetical case may occur to someone who is engaged in a piece of philosophical writing may not be something for which a particular *reason* can be given. We have already seen how important the role of

---

[41]"The Intentional Fallacy", *Sewanee Review,* Vol. LTV, 1946, pp. 468 ff.
[42]*Ibid.*

metaphor is in propelling on-going argument. The choice of examples, illustrations, jokes and hypothetical cases, is no less crucial in sending argument on its way. How could the selection of such devices be "accounted for"? Sometimes *interests* can be detected in such choices. Kant's writings draw on his knowledge of many of the sciences. Some of the idealists were knowledgeable about music and so talked of themes, harmony and discord. Ryle was keen on chess, Heidegger on poetry, and so on. It would be strange if a philosopher's non-philosophical interests failed to show themselves in some way in his writings. But is there a distinction between philosophical and non-philosophical interests any more than there is any clear cut divide between internal and external evidence in the context of interpreting literary texts? How are we to identify and weight the 'explanatory stratum' in the case of a philosophical text, and how much of it includes reference to the author's biography? How much biographical data can be deemed extraneous? It would certainly be relevant, in studying Kant's "Refutation of Idealism", to take into account his 'intention' to clear his position vis-à-vis those who were confusing his epistemology with that of Berkely. But knowing about his punctuality or having an acquaintance with the correspondence he had with his physician hardly throws light on his stress on time in the Transcendental Analytic. So, all in all, a philosopher's intention seems to be identifiable as "what he was trying to say". We do, in fact, often use the phrase "trying to say", "what I mean is...", in oral philosophical discussion. The intention is clarified in the very formulation thereof. In the case of the written text the intention is to be discovered within it.

Let us turn to another point. The anti-intentionalist speaks of "*the* text". And yet a text, even the 'final' one which results after the modifications made in several drafts, is not a stopper, but rather a cue which calls for interpretation. The historiographer's approach is somehow neglected in our study of philosophical texts except perhaps for those concerned with ancient Greek philosophy. Yet the way, say, in which the Hegelians studied Kant is clearly utterly different from that of Prichard, Strawson or Heidegger. Wherein lies *the* text? No doubt as in the case of Biblical scholarship, where the whole question of hermeneutics arose in the first place, "What X may himself be taken to have meant" and "What it may mean for us today" (and of course with the passage of time there can be no end of perspectives) might diverge radically. Notoriously it was fashionable in empiricist circles not so long ago to whitewash Berkeley as a phenomenalist of contemporary vintage, something which doubtless would have dismayed Berkeley beyond words.

Another thing. Is there anything parallel to "response to a literary work" in our reactions to a philosophical text? This is a tricky question. There is an unmistakeable personal dimension about our response to literature, both in the sense that we respond *as* persons, that is, totally; and we respond *to* something which is personal in that it bears the mark of the person who created it. To stress the iconic character of the work of art is to underplay this latter feature. But our ability to distinguish between individual styles is surely evidence of our recognition of the idiosyncratic, of the personal. This factor is, I think, also present in our response to different sorts of philosophic prose. We can recognise what is Cartesian or what is Kantian. The positivist grits his teeth in the face of a paragraph written by Heidegger. The metaphysically inclined are no less prone to do likewise these days in the face of a page of symbols purporting to present a 'model' or something that could be well be presented in good English (or French or what have you) prose. And why we do it, I venture to say, is because of the noticeable *omission* of that sense of personal statement that well-written philosophical prose gives us. Not, of course, that this is *enough*. The discriminating reader certainly brings to his understanding of a text criteria of 'soundness' relevant to the matters under discussion.

But we have yet to come to the point where the question about intention becomes most challenging. Wimsatt and Beardsley write: "For all the objects of our manifold experience, especially for the intellectual objects, for every unit, there is an action of the mind which cuts off roots, melts away context – or indeed we should never have objects or ideas or anything to talk about."[43] What Lazerowitz has been telling us is really this, that this cutting off of roots which we traditionally do in our scrutiny of the truth claims made by philosophers, has all along been a misguided procedure. Examine the roots and you find very common-or-garden things like wishes, hopes and fears, and you will forthwith cease to be bewitched by the seductive illusions which philosophers have been spinning before your eyes. While this may clear our minds of alleged lumber, (Lazerowitz thinks it definitely will), nature abhors a vacuum as the cliché has it, and the new illusions that take the place of the debunked ones may be a lot more "undesirable" than the original ones were. Twentieth-century 'enlightenment' has been accompanied by much that is frightening and terrible. A secular aseptic century has seen a resurgence of witchcraft, black magic, and the new crime of genocide, in many cases involving the use of the 'rational' instruments provided by recent technology. We are unable to do without "Ideenkleid" to use Husserl's useful term. The "Ideenkleid" provided by a seminal thinker is peculiarly his own. But because we share a common intersubjective world of meanings it is not opaque to the rest of us.

We are led once again to the distinction between the *Naturwissenschaften* and *Geisteswissenschaften*. As we move away from the symbolic constructs of the former into the symbolic worlds created by artists and philosophers we move into a sphere where 'intention' cannot be discounted except at the peril of misunderstanding. But 'intention' must not be identified in a reductive manner with the regressive and the infantile. Living thought, above all, has its being

---

[43] *Ibid.*

betwixt the was and the shall be. Thinking has its own archaeology and its own teleology, to borrow the useful terminology of Paul Ricoeur.[44] But we are in a quandary about explaining how they are related. To speak of a dialectic of the two, polarizes unduly. To speak of creativity as, since the time of Bergson, it is natural for writers in the French tradition to do, seems to over-mystify. The philosopher, like all writers, generates meaning through the symbols he employs. We have already noticed in our analysis of metaphor that the nature of philosophical discourse is a lot less linear than most philosophers have thought it to be. The dynamism of thought, what Tetens called quite literally *Denkkraft*,[45] is fed from many sources and, in turn, reaches out in a genuine *poiesis* or making, a making which is also a doing. In anthropology, which is firmly situated among the *Geisteswissenschaften*, the skilled field-worker learns to correlate the aerial, the pedestrian, and the subterranean views.[46] That is to say, he has his own overarching hypotheses, his day-to-day field-work, taking into account also the role of geographical factors, and does not fail to remember the importance of geology. An analogous association of skills is required by the adventurer in metaphilosophy, and I do not use this word in any narrow sense.

The Freudian approach is subversive in so far as it confines us to the subterranean. But not all ideas surge up. Some beckon. It also introduces a new myth, the possibility of "the real" minus *Ideenkleid,* a myth which the psychoanalyst in his clinical work, operating with a standard and idealised conception of the 'normal', probably *requires*. But it is a sobering thought to reflect that Don Quixote died not from illusions but out of sanity. As for those who incorporated Freud's insights in their philosophizing they tended to think that if a concept satisfied an emotional need this necessarily debarred it from serving an explanatory purpose. But words like 'dynamic', 'creative' and 'vital' cannot be debunked so easily. There is often a *kinship* between the satisfying and the satisfactory, although we should not count too much on it. After the unmasking, we take up our lives as before. One persona is exchanged for another. The familiar remains familiar and becomes an avenue to our exploration of the unfamiliar. Freud's work focused on the *disguise* of thought and so he saw the topography of the psychical in terms of the polarity between the latent and the manifest. To be engaged in exploring the language of philosophy as we are in this study is to be engaged in a different task – that of finding out how thought progressively defines itself and becomes more and more articulate. We began this chapter with mention of a bogey, the bogey of subterranean influence. The discussion now brings us face to face with another

---

[44] *Freud and Philosophy: an essay on interpretation,* Yale, 1970.
[45] Vide *Philosophical Essays on Human Nature,* 1777, Ch. 4.
[46] I owe this analogy to the late Nirmal Kumar Bose, India's most outstanding anthropologist in this century.

bogey, the bogey of the approximation of philosophy to poetry. If philosophising is a form of *poiein,* if it issues in the creation of symbolic structures born out of man's total psychical resources, can we at all distinguish it from poetry? This bogey must occupy us next.

CHAPTER VII

Philosophy and Poetry

In an early number of analysis (1933) A.J. Ayer engaged in a discussion with C.A. Mace about "The Genesis of Metaphysics", arguing that metaphysical nonsense was rather the product of linguistic confusion "than an attempt to express poetically what could not literally be said".[1] It pinpoints two familiar ways of discrediting metaphysical discourse, the second of which we shall be concerned with in what follows. Many of the idealist philosophers, and also Bergson, were confronted with the charge of approximating to poetry at the turn of this century, the assumption being that no self-respecting philosopher should allow himself to be seduced away from argument and led into the miasma of poetic expression. The assumption was there even before the positivists joined the attack, wielding their weapon of literal significance. Today the divide between literature and philosophy is taken for granted in the English-speaking world. I may mention a more recent illustration of this. In a broadcast interview Iris Murdoch made the pronouncement that "when one is writing philosophy, one is writing something which is more like science than like literature".[2] She went on to express the opinion, surprising for one who is a novelist herself, that "literature mystifies and philosophy clarifies". The opinion is all the more extraordinary for its superficiality considering that Miss Murdoch is not only a contemporary novelist but a classical scholar familiar no less with the dramas of Sophocles and Euripides than with the works of Plato and Aristotle. What has happened to philosophy in the twentieth century? The most obvious answer is that it has become thoroughly professionalised and that this professionalisation has somehow or other reinforced the separation of philosophy from the domain of letters and situated it, whenever possible, in the domain of formulae. To leaf through the pages of all too many philosophy journals is to find them un-readable. The skill required is not the ability to read prose so much as the ability to operate with symbols and calculi. The loss of unified sensibility bemoaned by T.S. Eliot has led not only to obscurity in poetry but to aridity in philosophy.

To gaze back whence we have come may not be considered very relevant to

---

[1] Mentioned by Ayer in *Part of My Life*, O.U.P. Paperback, 1977, p. 151.
[2] Vide *The Listener*, 27.4.1978.

where we are right now. It only finds relevance, to develop the geographical metaphor, if a suspicion begins to dawn on us that we have somewhere lost the way. Not to mention the epic literature outside the western tradition, no one can deny the philosophical content of Homer's and Hesiod's epics. The pre-Socratics wrote in didactic poems. The great dramatists wrote of the perennial themes of fate, birth and death, the very same themes which also occupied the philosophers. The same dimension of depth is found in each, a common preoccupation with the poignant contrast between actual and ideal, a striving for wholeness in the teeth of the fragmentariness of life. If the dramas are weighted more on the side of terror and fantasy, this can be accounted for not only by the hard facts of political life but by the exigencies of dramatic action and the mythic aura which is more proper to the conjuring of spectacle than to the presentation of argument. Fate is a very potent agency in Greek literature, the limit that curbs the destinies of men and keeps their aspirations within the boundaries appropriate to creatures moulded out of clay. The philosopher does not *need* to speak overtly of *hybris*. The awareness of limit is built into the awareness of all who *think,* whether they be mathematicians or philosophers. The Platonic Dialogues were a synthesis of philosophy and drama and in Cicero's time were actually acted on the stage by Roman intellectuals.

It was Aristotle who invented the philosophical treatise and thereby initiated an *estrangement* between philosophy and literature. Thereafter, with the notable exception of Lucretius' didactic poem *De Rerum Nature* (whose poetic appeal, even for the Latinist is minimal), the business of philosophy was taken to be with discourse, and with discourse alone. To borrow a phrase from Clement of Alexandria, we must "pass to intellectual objects". In the meantime, literature went its own way, pursuing meaning through symbol, myth, imagery, allegory, irony and paradox. Apart from the lone exception of the essay, it could be taken for granted that literature is not genuinely discursive and, among literary genres, poetry very evidently not discursive at all. And yet a critic like Cleanth Brooks can speak of poetry as "covert metaphysics".[3] Perhaps philosophy and poetry have more in common than meets the eye, even though Cleanth Brooks adds, "The poem need not, and ought not to, aspire to become explicit metaphysics."[4]

Both philosophers and poets, as T.S. Eliot puts it, "wrestle with words and meanings". The amount of wrestling that the poet is engaged in has usually been underplayed by those not involved in the craft of writing poetry. For example, Ricoeur thinks that in poetry "the unfettered extensions of meaning spring free".[5] Those who see more clearly the kinship between poet and prophet than that between poet and philosopher detect in each an inspiration

---

[3]"Metaphor and the function of Criticism" in *Spiritual Problems in Contemporary Literature,* edited by Stanley Romaine Hopper, pp. 127—37.
[4]*Ibid.*
[5]*The Rule of Metaphor,* p. 261.

which infuses events with new meanings, a capacity which is above all intuitive. The poet has, no doubt, sometimes donned the mantle of a Jeremiah. But he need not do so, having, as he does, a mantle of his own. The root, for both poet and philosopher, is a kind of "inquietude", the term Condillac uses to describe what he feels to be the starting point of mental phenomena.[6] 'When Coleridge finds a certain restlessness in imagination he is referring perhaps to the same thing. It plumbs far deeper than the cramps, puzzles, riddles, logical disquiets *et al.* of the linguistic analyst. To be involved in the craft of writing poetry or the shaping of metaphysical discourse is to *experience* the momentum of thought. To say that the momentum does not depend on wholly rational processes is not as near the mark as to say that the process is by no means a wholly cerebral one. Coleridge, of whom more will be said later, has much that is challenging to say on this theme. Writing of a poet in his own day he says, "he has no native Passion, because he is not a Thinker – and has probably weakened his Intellect by the haunting Fear of becoming extravagant."[7] The great Poet and Thinker are alike possessed of 'native Passion'. This may read strangely in the context of the eighteenth-century polarisation of reason and passion typified especially in the difference in temperament between Voltaire and Rousseau.

But Voltaire surely writes with passion, and passion armed with irony and wit is perhaps the most potent of all. The strict rationalist often makes a virtue of necessity. This point is made neatly by Edward Young: "Men of cold complexions are very apt to mistake a want of vigour in their imaginations for a delicacy of taste in their judgements."[8] So it is a misunderstanding of the nature of poetry and philosophy that has been partly responsible for the view which sees the two as polar to each other. The poet wrestles with words no less than the philosopher does, and the philosopher finds that words are poor counters unless he is caught up in winds of thought which challenge his powers of navigation and assist him in venturing forth. When a writer possesses both form and *power* we have someone whom both poet and philosopher admire. It is worth remembering that both Coleridge and Heidegger are great admirers of Pindar. In Pindar's poetry there is a triumphant fusion of elevated thought, highly figurative language and command of form – the whole work resonant with Homeric echoes. An inner logic is at work in Pindar's poetry, but it is a logic infused with *power*. Heidegger finds profoundly metaphysical themes at work in the Olympian Ode IX, 100 and the Pythian Ode II, 72, a passionate concern with Being, a Being whose essence it is to appear. There is a world of difference in finding all that there is in the world of appearance and saying that it is the nature of what *is* to show itself, that is, to appear. It is this latter insight that Heidegger finds embodied in Pindar's poetry. What Maritain speaks of as

---
[6] *Extrait Raisonné.*
[7] Letter to William Sotheby (10 September 1802) in which he comments on William Lisle Bowles¹ "The Spirit of Navigation".
[8] *A Discourse on Lyric Poetry,* 1728.

the "primordial intelligible density of being"[9] is experienced by both poet and philosopher. Both likewise experience a poignant sense of inadequacy of meaning, a limitation which pervades (one could even say infects) our entire being. Whatever the metaphysician or the poet accomplishes is accomplished in the very teeth of this inadequacy. The unspeaking mystery which instructs us[10] does so through the book of nature and the inmost powers of man himself, including that concourse of minds which all who wrestle with language are familiar with. Both philosopher and poet develop cues to meaning. To see this is to see the inappropriateness of looking upon the philosophic task as a working upon data, still less as an activity which terminates with stoppers. The disciplines which deal with data are the sciences. The false polarisation between facts and illusions, which locates metaphysical systems and poetry among the latter, stems from a blindness (and deafness) to cues of meaning.

The common ground between philosophy and poetry in fact opens up the more we dwell on it, and this dwelling can be taken both literally and metaphorically. In the greatest philosophical writing (and I am here thinking of metaphysics) ideas incandesce and concepts become images infused with mythic power. In the case of Nietzsche, moreover, the writing has an inspirational dimension. Both poet and philosopher engage in a self-distancing operation (highly personal though it be) detached from the spheres of manipulation and contrivance. This of course would be denied by the Marxist, because the Marxist viewpoint, though philosophical, is essentially anti-metaphysical. While the 'poetic' element in philosophy has been generally neglected, and some of the reasons for this can be found in our earlier discussion of reason and imagination,[11] the philosophic content of much poetry has been given due recognition. I only mention here a few examples by way of illustration of a point which is fairly obvious. Dante and Milton are regarded as possessing an imagination generated by thought, a phrase used by literary critics and which is philosophically tantalising. No one can read these two great poets without being aware of the sinews of their thought. It was Milton who coined the phrase "the mind as its own place" which speaks across centuries in rejoinder to those who talk of "the mind and its place in nature". The student of pantheism needs to read not only the philosophers but Wordsworth's "Tintern Abbey". The conflict between French atheism and Platonic idealism is set forth in Shelley's "Prometheus Unbound". The theme of immortality occupies *In Memoriam* no less than it does the *Phaedo*. The debt of Wordsworth's *Lyrical Ballads* to Hartley's philosophy of mind or of Coleridge to Neo-Platonism is well known to students of literature. Only those who reduce the poetic imagination to image-making can miss the ratiocinative

---

[9] J. Maritain, *Existence and existent*, pp. 29-30.
[10] I borrow this phrase from Karl Rahner.
[11] Vide Chapter 2.

content that poetry has, a content which is as distinctive in Wordsworth's "To daffodils" as it is in Browning's "Bishop Blougram's apology". It may be more evident in the latter. But this does not mean that Wordsworth was less of a *thinker* than Browning was.

The relation between contemporary poetry and philosophy is a theme in itself. Beginning with Wordsworth's plea for "one very language of men" English poetry has been progressively concerned with the significance of the everyday. Much of contemporary poetry deals with the commonplace just as much of contemporary philosophy is fascinated by what it calls ordinary language. The hazards on each side are, respectively, bathos and triviality. If poetic diction has, for many, become a museum piece, so has "philosophical language". The idea of elevated thoughts occasions all too often these days mirth rather than dismay. And yet current language can be heightened to a degree, as in Hopkins' poetry, and the prose of philosophy can be not merely felicitous but magnificent, as in some of Bertrand Russell's writings.

The age of anxiety[12] reflected in Auden's poetry finds an eloquent voice in the novels of Sartre and Camus and perhaps rather less eloquently, outside fiction, in existentialist philosophical prose. Existentialist philosophical thought can be seen as in large part centred on the plea for a unified sensibility which the eighteenth century broke up into faculties and the twentieth century into the Ego and the Id. Both Robbe-Grillet and Gilbert Ryle are intent on abolishing the alleged "myth of depth", the former with his view of the novel as an interpretation-free fabric of textures and the latter with his analysis of the dispositional. One final example can be added. Some world-views are organised around a certain image (the etymology of 'Weltanschauung' gives a warrant for this), and those who compose variations on the theme of alienation in our times have in fact built their systems on the image of struggle. Here concrete imagination gives rise to a philosophic system based on what is believed to be a pervasive pattern in experience.

But it would be unfair to give the impression that there is not much which distinguishes philosophy from poetry. While many poets employ archetypal imagery the philosopher's choice of imagery in the modern period (ancient Greek philosophy is full of archetypal imagery) seems to be of a different kind. But there is at least one major exception to this – the archetypal image of vision which runs right through from Plato to the most brash of contemporary questionings of the form "Do you see the point?" While much of Plato's imagery is archetypal, that of the linguistic analysts is certainly not, with the possible exception of the 'therapy' idea which is hoary indeed. But the hoary *need* not be archetypal.

In poetic language, as Valéry puts it, a pendulum oscillates between sound

---

[12]*Vide* Chapter X on "Existentialism and Literature" in my *The Existentialist Outlook*, Orient Longman, 1973.

and sense. Coleridge goes further and maintains that sound provides "the lyrical initiative" for poetry. While there are thinkers like Simone Weil and Martin Heidegger who lay special stress on listening rather than seeing, we do not usually study passages of philosophical writing for their sonorous prose (perhaps it would be better if we did) but for their meaning. No one has thought of formulating an aphorism about philosophy parallel to Archibald McLeish's one about poetry. In philosophical statement the sense, rather than the sound, is our prime concern. The ambiguity or, in Tillyard's language, obliquity, which can add to the delight a poem gives the reader, is taken as a fault in philosophic prose. I do not refer here to the legitimate *Spielraum* of philosophical metaphors which was discussed earlier, a matter which, on our view, is of critical importance in the vindication of metaphysical writing against a crude kind of positivist criticism. Something akin to the tensive quality of poetic meaning is present at the nodal points in philosophic discourse where argument is propelled by metaphor. But the tension is resolved in the thrust of argument, nor does it become a focus of delight. In fact the philosopher may ruefully be aware of the extent to which this particular factor is absent as an outcome of his efforts. We are led to the point where we see, we understand, and sometimes we are convinced. This is perhaps to put a charitable complexion on the state of affairs, and lacquer over the cracks with consoling words. Much of contemporary philosophical writing deals with painful matters, with perplexity, with the unravelling of knots which refuse to be unravelled, with the bumping of heads against limits which refuse even to bend. How rarely we are delighted! But we are not supposed to be. The fact is that a great deal of twentieth-century *poetry* does not delight either. We churn away, not in primeval oceans but in the puddles in our own backyards. Not Primavera in all her pristine innocence, but the nightmare images of Belsen and Hiroshima haunt our dreams. And so they should if we have any conscience at all.

The question about delight is perhaps parasitic on another matter, the iconic character of the work of art. Now, though the philosophic text is verbal, we cannot speak of it as a verbal icon. As a work, an opus, a symbolic construction, it is essentially discursive, not presentational. But it *is* possible to read a philosophical text with an attitude close to the aesthetic. One can read some of the Platonic Dialogues or at least many passages in them, in this frame of mind. But the frisson we get, say, in reading Bertrand Russell's "A Free Man's Worship" where thoughts are certainly elevated although not in a conventional or orthodox mould, is deemed, most would say, irrelevant to our understanding of the text. Perhaps only in studying the total corpus of a philosopher's work, where we attempt to characterise it in the most general terms, we acquire, if we go deep enough, a certain totality of impression which is akin to our response to the iconic in the work of art.

The attitude of philosophers to poets shows a wide scatter. Thomas Aquinas, in commenting on Aristotle's *Posterior Analytics*, ranks poetry only above sophistic which in turn is ranked lowest in a gradation from syllogistic certitude downwards. Catholic thought, as shown both in Aquinas and in Maritain, sees the source of poetry in the pre-conscious life of the intellect, and finds therein a characteristic integrity. The pre-conscious, on this view, it is necessary to note, is not the same as the Freudian unconscious, participating as it does in the extended life of the ratiocinative part of man. The modern philosopher, exiled from the possibility of intellectual intuition, has, on rare occasions, envied the poet his gift of concrete intuition. Such a one was Whitehead. Whitehead believes that the philosopher ought to study the poets, masters as they are of *concrete intuition*.[13] The intuitive character of poetic truth is stressed by Schopenhauer, Croce, Bergson and Langer. Kierkegaard is perhaps unique in often using the words 'poet' and 'thinker' interchangeably, ambivalent though his own attitude to poetry was. He says: "... The author... calls himself... a peculiar kind of poet or thinker, who 'without authority' has nothing new to bring, but would read through yet once more the original text of the individual human existence-relationship – the old, well-known, handed down from the fathers – if possible in a more heartfelt way."[14] To Kierkegaard, existential neutrality is as impossible for the philosopher as it is for the poet. Philosophy *becomes* poetry in so far as it attains the subjectively and passionately appropriated truths that the poet attains. The poet, through what appears to be a highly disengaged and iconic form of utterance, through resplendent images, succeeds in communicating a level of experience where thought and feeling coincide. Kierkegaard himself chose a more indirect and refracted form of communication, the parable and the fable. While paradox is resolved and reconciled in the poetic symbol, it remains stark and unresolved for existential reflection. Home viator has to leave behind the temporary resting-places of romantic imagination as, pilgrimwise, he goes on his way. Figurative writing is not to be 'enjoyed'. It is a vehicle of self-understanding which is to find its proper terminus in decision. As a spokesman of paradox, Kierkegaard is more radical in his claim to truth than the analogical reasoner can dare to be. For Kierkegaard falsity is "not being in the Truth". Passionate appropriation is matched by the passionate self-giving of Revelation. Only thus, for Kierkegaard, can finite and infinite meet. They meet, that is to say, not in poetic symbol, but in the moment of prayer.

The rest of the discussion will centre round the work of two thinkers, who, to my mind, probe most deeply into the nature of the relation between philosophy and poetry, Coleridge, the poet who felt himself gripped by Kant's transcendental philosophy "as with a giant's hand", and Heidegger, the philosopher who devoted many of his lectures to themes derived from the poets, and whose relation to Hölderlin proved crucial for his own thought.

---

[13]Vide *Science and the Modern World,* Ch. V.
[14]*For Self-examination and Judge for Yourselves,* Princeton, 1944, p. 5.

Both, moreover, experienced the dilemma facing the man who pursues two vocations, that of philosopher and poet.

Coleridge is remarkable for reaching his philosophical conclusions, not so much through the reading of academic philosophy, although there is evidence of the breadth of his reading, as through his experience of his own craft as a poet and his response to the work of his fellow poets. The philosophical content of his thought is threefold, his neo-Platonism, his opposition to Hartleian epistemology, and his transcendentalism. His Platonism shows itself in his belief that "like can only be known by like",[15] and his sense that the light of common day is not enough. For Coleridge, the pursuit of truth is directed towards the ideal. The pursuit can never terminate with the oracles of the market-place. His encounter with Cudworth's *True Intellectual System* in May 1795 gave him the stimulus to reject Hartleian associationism and to separate fancy and imagination in a way which could make intelligible the "... lofty imaginings, that are peculiar to, and definitive of, the poet". By the time he left for Germany in 1798 to compile material for a biography of Lessing, he was already in contact with Wordsworth's mind and art, and sufficiently in recoil from British empiricism to be receptive to the philosophical thinking of the Continent. What excited him most in Kant's philosophy was no doubt the productive imagination of the Schematism. But whatever he discovered in Kant was transmuted in the crucible of his own thinking. Coleridge goes beyond the faculty framework of Kant's analysis of mind and thinks of the various operations of the mind in terms of interrelated *powers*. This finds expression not in statements phrased in academically correct language but in his letters e.g. "My opinion is this – that deep Thinking is attainable only by a man of deep Feeling...."[16] and "... a great poet must be implicitè if not explicitè, a profound metaphysician."[17]

The key is the imagination (not fancy), which is the esemplastic power which synthesises thought, feeling and poetic form. The detaching of fancy from imagination frees the latter from connection with fictions and illusions which depend on the aggregative capacities of the mind. These aggregative capacities are not underplayed by Coleridge, but the source of creativity is not to be found among them. The new cannot result from ringing the changes on the contents of the mind in a mechanical manner. The poet is essentially one who possesses both energy and depth of thought. Coleridge does lapse into teleological language in order to bring out the non-mechanical character of the movement of poetic thought. Time and again he returns to the idea of power and energy. A great poet like Shakespeare possesses the power "of so carrying on the Eye of the Reader as to make him almost lose the consciousness of words... without any *anatomy* of description...but with the sweetness and easy

---

[15] *The Statesman's Manual*, p. 39.
[16] Letter to Thomas Poole, 23 March 1801.
[17] Letter to William Sotheby, 13 July 1802.

movement of nature".[18] In view of "the dimness of the intellectual eye"[19] the total energies of the human mind need to be enlisted, with the key role located in the 'co-adunating' power of the imagination. Coleridge's remedy in the face of the limits of pure reason is clearly very different from Kant's. Philosophers have notoriously distrusted the *saltus,* the leap, of thought. But as early as 1810 Coleridge uses the image of the leap in a very suggestive way. Leaping requires the force of gravitation; but we leap "by a power counteracting first, and then using the force of gravitation...."[20] The *Biographia Literaria* elaboration of this image goes on to analyse the process as involving that of two powers at work, active and passive, along with an intermediate faculty which is both active and passive, i.e. the imagination. In *Table Talk,* years later, in 1833,[21] he maintains that "... the higher intellectual powers can only act through a corresponding energy of the lower". The language of active and passive, higher and lower was common in Coleridge's time, and like many of his contemporaries, Coleridge found in the metaphor of the organic a way of combining them all. But what is at stake in all the discussion, and this is the interesting point for our theme, is *not* the choice between the real and the illusory. Beyond these there is the ideal. It is the film of the familiar which all too often *is* the illusory. What a poet like Wordsworth does is to awaken us to be novelty and freshness of the everyday and in one and the same act to awaken our mind to the ideal. The "unenlivened generalizing understanding", and the "self-circling energies of the reason" are alike incapable of doing this for us.

Coleridge's best-known account of the symbolic process comes in *The Statesman's Manual:*"...a symbol is characterized by the translucence of the special in the individual, or of the general in the special, or of the universal in the general. Above all by the translucence of the eternal through and in the temporal. It always partakes of the reality which it renders intelligible; and while it enunciates the whole, abides itself as a living part in that unity, of which it is the representative."[22] Taking this passage along with its immediate context, Coleridge is here engaged not in debunking our conceptual powers but is suggesting how they are fed, and how reason is not in fact cut off (as Kant thinks it is) from that sensible nutriment which alone can give it content. The following makes this more explicit:[23] "The Reason...as the integral *spirit* of the regenerated man, reason substantiated and vital... without being either the SENSE, the UNDERSTANDING, or the IMAGINATION contains all three

---

[18]*Notebooks,* March 1805.
[19]*Lecture on Romeo and Juliet,* 12 December 1811.
[20]*Notebooks,* 111 3708 (10 March 1810). The image is further elaborated in *Biographia Literaria* 1, 85-6, (pub. 1817).
[21]20 August 1833.
[22]December 1816.
[23]Quoted by J.S. Hill in *Imagination 'n Coleridge,* 1978, pp. 155-6.

within itself, even as the mind contains its thoughts and is present in and through them all; or as the expression pervades the different features of an intelligent countenance." The idea expressed in this passage reaches out to Dilthey's exploration of the mind and its powers a century later. Of course he puts us in a dilemma. If reason is so expanded, and even further, so as to include what he himself called "Truths below the surface". We must need give up the distinction between rational and irrational. At the end of a century which was "the Epoch of the Understanding and the Senses" and when over-cerebral products of Reason whether in verse or philosophy were in bad odour, Coleridge was daring enough to suggest an alternative, one that was far closer to Dilthey than to Kant. He thinks of reason as a dynamic power, striving for wholeness, one which neither repudiates nor regulates the matrix out of which it issues, not an abstraction, but energetic and vital. It is surely out of such a capacity that both poetry and philosophy are born. In his *Biographia Literaria* which was published a year after the *Statesman's Manual* (although written earlier than the latter), imagination is still given the *formative* power, and back of it is life, the "principle of individuation". At any rate a firm negative answer now emerges to Coleridge's question to Godwin years earlier,[24] "...Is logic the Essence of thinking?"

Among the questions that remain are first of all this. If all the powers of mind are interrelated, it may be thought (and J.L. Lowes and Lascelles Abercrombie are of this opinion) that the distinction on which Coleridge laid such stress, that between fancy and imagination, ceases to have much point. But the passages where he elaborates on the image of the leap bring out the *interlocking* of powers (rather than their identity) which thinking, especially poetic thinking, involves. The second is a matter which Coleridge as a philosopher-poet (or poet-philosopher) is aware of and treats in passing but not, very understandably, in a systematic way, that is the relation of *bios* and *logos*. The dynamism of thought is the form of articulation of *bios* which is peculiar to man. Coleridge is Platonist enough to think of *logos* as an order which is echoed in man's own creative powers. The rootedness of art in life is possible because of the rootedness of life in nature. Coleridge's answer to the second question (paradoxical though this may seem) is provided most clearly by Wordsworth. The key to the relation between *bios* and *logos* is the insight that man is nature's priest. But nature itself points beyond, and this is why the rich symbolism which nature provides leads both poet and philosopher into a realm where we seem to be left with only the resources of intuition. Coleridge's rejoinder to Kant at this point is that he is not speaking of *intellectual* intuition but an intuition, or rather a concrete imagination, made possible by man's total psychic endowments. Herein lies the clue to the passion both of the thinker and of the poet. Coleridge sees the reconciling of philosophy and poetry as

---

[24]September 1800.

primarily of benefit to the latter, for it is with the analysis of the poetic imagination that he is primarily concerned. But when he reminds us that "we cannot reason without imagination"[25] this cannot fail to be of profound importance to the philosopher. Coleridge sees in imagination a principle of *growth*, the key to the momentum of the non-aggregating work of thought. He thereby opens up a different path to the analysis of innovative thinking, as distinct from the chewing the cud model of the associationists, where thinking is confined to the contents acquired through the senses, as from the Kantian, the pursuit of intellectual carrots which the categorial understanding is ill-equipped to reach, or the Hegelian locating of the moving and the vital in the factor of contradiction. Innovative thinking, in both philosophy and poetry, is made possible first and foremost by the fact that man's powers are not in water-tight compartments. These powers may not always be in harmony, but the highest outreaches of thinking, although in no way *reducible* to the rest, yet owe their driving energy to *all* the powers and not just to intellect. Here is Coleridge's reply to the thinkers of the Enlightenment. It is out of this total endowment of psychic powers that man has the capacity to perceive the translucence of the particular. What a religious temperament sees as bearing the divine signature a more secular mind can at least see as bearing the imprint of the universal. And from there it is but a small step to nature mysticism.

Heidegger is not a nature mystic. If there are at times traces in Coleridge of an attempt to seek out a post-Christian *logos*. Heidegger is very consciously exploring a pre-Christian *logos*, that is, a dimension which is profoundly Greek. For Heidegger there is a primordial bonding of beings the articulation of which is set us as a task, whether as philosophers or poets. While Coleridge forges a path distinct from the concept-spinning of the rationalists and the mechanistic analogies of the empiricists, Heidegger's endeavour is, in comparison, catalysmic. He is attempting nothing less than to find a way out of *nihilism*. There is yet much that unites them. Both are conscious that man has lost his wholeness, and that the thinker, whether he be poet or philosopher, is engaged in a passionate recovery of that which has been lost. An element of nostalgia is perhaps built into modern consciousness. Both have experienced, from within, thinking on the move; for Coleridge the movement of poetic imagination, the whole creative process, and for Heidegger the impetus of philosophic questioning, the wonder that leads to radical searching. Both were deeply committed to the task of *revivifying* language. If Coleridge and Wordsworth react against artificial diction, Heidegger writes in the consciousness of the *decay* of language. The twentieth century has witnessed the trivialising of language through propaganda, the facile formulations of the copy-writer, the bathetic expressions of the popular song-writer, the edging out of verbal skills by a host of mechanical contrivances. But words can only lose

---

[25] *The Notebooks of Samuel Taylor Coleridge*, 111, 357.

their power when man himself has undergone a radical impoverishment of being. That metaphysics itself should be unfashionable is the most potent evidence of this impoverishment. To say all this is to say that there is much more to link Coleridge and Heidegger than common indebtedness to Kant and to German romanticism.

The take-off point for Heidegger is his conviction that human existence is not conceptually analysable, and yet that it is with human existence that the elucidation of Being must begin. This in itself indicates the need for a new path in the exploration of language, a path other than the contemporary fashionable one which assumes that to deal with language philosophically is to deal with concepts simpliciter. Secondly, although Heidegger's entire work may (in the context of positivist denigration of metaphysics) appear as a strenuous attempt directed towards rehabilitating metaphysics, this is not the way that Heidegger himself sees his work at all. The implicit dialogue he has with other philosophers is not with those of positivist leanings but with those who were metaphysicians in the grand manner. Heidegger saw his own path as proceeding *beyond* metaphysics, more in terms of a growth of illumination rather than as linear progress towards a goal. Thirdly, there is a further difference between the way in which the student of Heidegger's thought is likely to differ from Heidegger's own understanding of what he was about. The theological overtones of his thought are unmistakeable. At times they are so persistent that Heidegger seems to be engaging in a kind of secularised meta-theology. Heidegger, however, was always impatient with those who came to this conclusion. A simplified way of putting it would be to say that for Heidegger the philosopher is primarily a *thinker*, whereas the theologian labours within the context of faith. The identification of the concept of God with that of Being was the achievement of the religious thought of the Middle Ages. But this is not an identification which is to be found in Heidegger. If we take these three considerations together, a flight from the purely conceptual, from *intellectus,* a desire to shake off the shackles of metaphysical systems, and a desire to steer clear of theology, what emerges is a temper which is peculiarly *capable* of finding affinity between the philosopher and the poet. The route is not the same as that of Coleridge, but their ways are strikingly parallel. While Coleridge's poetic sensibility is nourished by philosophy, Heidegger's reflection as a philosophical thinker is fed by the concreteness of imagination which he finds above all in the poets. While Coleridge glimpsed a daylight Platonic vision in Cudworth, Heidegger entered into a twilight zone when he first came across *Menschheitsdämmerung,* an anthology of Expressionist poems edited by Kurt Pintus, and published in 1921. Both were to find the image of depth more congenial than that of height; both were to be fascinated by the interplay of light and dark (perhaps in a way which only those familiar with woodland scenery can); both carried on an implicit conversation with a vast range of pioneer thinkers from Pindar through to Kant; both had an extraordinarily developed sense of the ontological weight of words. Both were baffled by the riddle of human existence.

It is not until fairly late in Heidegger's corpus of writings that the impact of the poets, and the appeal of poetry, can be fully felt. We find him, as a philosopher, first of all struggling with language in certain characteristic ways. It is no easy task to sort these out in any intelligible fashion, but for the sake of simplicity we can perhaps single out the following: (a) the use of etymology to discover primal meanings; (b) the importance given to prepositions; (c) the use of metaphor; (d) thinking as a dialogue with one's predecessors; and (e) the use of paradox. Somewhere amidst all these Heidegger hopes to be able to illuminate man's situation in Being. Poetry does not come in as something to be resorted to when all else has failed, but rather he finds that the poet is *already* making his furrows in very similar fields. Philosopher and poet, as it were, greet each other, working as they do in neighbouring territories with soil, rocks, winds and sky equally familiar to each. We must, however, first examine the above pointers in turn. And they are no more than pointers.

To look to etymology as a cue to meaning is very evidently the very opposite strategy to examining current usage. Language for Heidegger is *not* a tool. He would say that those who think of language in terms of instrumentality are those who manipulate, who debase it. To such, the very word "Being" has no meaning. Heidegger believes there is a profound relation between the interrogation of Being and the origin of language. It is almost as if he believed that heaven lies about us in our infancy, where the infancy in question is that of speech. To stress etymology is, moreover, to stress that language is already *there,* whatever our present locutions may be. Or, to adopt a different idiom, language games may presuppose forms of life, but *behind* both of these is language. We do not reify language in saying this. Rather we recognise the historical character of the whole enterprise of using language. Etymology, Heidegger believes, is the chief, although not the only clue, to this history. To think of language as a tool is to assume that man has *invented* language, which, to Heidegger is a mistake. To retrieve the perennial freshness of language is particularly important for the philosopher, because layer upon layer of meanings have accumulated during the course of the history of philosophy. What we have today are words which are 'left-overs',[26] and with this we should not be content. This is why Heidegger explores Greek and German roots with such care, often arriving at insights which dismay specialists in both languages. How else, asks Heidegger, are we to probe behind the veils of meaning which successive generations have set up?

This whole stress on etymology is no doubt part of a German quest for "was gründlich ist". It has been a target of criticism from many quarters, the logical

---

[26] A word Heidegger used in his *Physics* Seminar in 1940. Vide Heidegger: *Through Phenomenology to Thought,* by William J. Richardson, S.J. Nijhoff, 1967, p. 497.

positivist line of attack being taken as read. Is Heidegger not pursuing a will-o'-the-wisp; is he not making the mistake of looking for *the* meaning, when we would do better to go along with Alice and agree that words mean what we choose them to mean? The trouble is that Alice's alternative seems too extreme. In other words, Heidegger along with Wittgenstein, seems to be warning us that language has limits. The difference is that where Wittgenstein finds the limits in use (an idea which doesn't take in sufficiently how, say, a great writer can *stretch* use, or find a *new* use) Heidegger finds the limit in the *root*. But limit so conceived, for him, is not merely source but *re*source, that is, a clue for fresh thinking. So we need to beware looking on Heidegger's etymological method as regressive in, say, the way Freud's is. We are to drink at the spring (die Quelle) in order to refresh ourselves. That is, in order to go forward. To be alive to the prompting of etymology, moreover, is to be safeguarded against impiety, the impiety of imagining that man is the shaper and master of language. Ernst Junger speaks sympathetically of this procedure: "He lifts a word while it slumbers silently, fresh and in full sprout, and he lifts it from the humus of the woods."[27]

There are others, though, who view it less charitably. Karl Löwith charges Heidegger with reducing philosophy to verbal play, "ein Glasperlenspiel mit Worten".[28] B. Allemann[29] calls Heidegger's stress on the individual word a type of pointillisme, not that this epithet in itself suggests a criticism. But at a time when those working in semantics and linguistics stress the *sentence* as the unit of meaning, the description of his method as pointilliste is certainly intended to be pejorative. The etymological method has also been pulled apart in T.W. Adorno's *Jargon der Eigentlichkeit* (1964), and mercilessly satirised in Günter Grass's novel *Hundejahre*. But, all the criticisms apart, it is a method which should not be divorced from the backdrop of German philological speculations from the time of Herder onwards, the interest of German speaking intellectuals in word play (mentioned earlier in the context of Freud and Wittgenstein), and Jung's concern with the archetypal. Archetypal imagery, which engages a whole school of literary critics, has affinities with etymology. No one with an ear for the resonances of words can simply write off Heidegger's explorations of Be-ing and a host of cognate terms.

The second pointer, the care bestowed on prepositions, is tied up with Heidegger's appeal to etymology. If the import of the latter is not so much "Look, this is what is meant", as "Look, this what *was* meant", we are left free to interpret words in new ways. This is made possible through a detaching of roots from prefixes and suffixes, breaking up compounds, and a reassembling of the parts in ways found to be insightful. There is perhaps no other

[27] *Martin Heidegger in Conversation*, ed. by Richard Wisser. Eng. tr., p. 14.
[28] *Denker in dürftiger Zeit*, p. 15. (The analogy of a game with glass pearls is taken from a novel by Hermann Hesse where the game is likened to a pseudo-scientific substitute for art.)
[29] *Hölderlin und Heidegger*, p. 108.

philosopher who is as inventive as Heidegger is in the use of prepositions, whether it be "hören auf", "Mitsein", or "vor-liegen lassen", the reader is affected uncannily, brought up short by the shock of something new and, at the same time, made to ponder over the implications of simple words whose ordinary uses he knows very well. When these alternative prepositional gambits are attached to one and same root we are invited, for example, to examine the difference between "andenken", "durchdenken", and "bedenken". Dwelling on prepositions shows up, moreover, how vital is the phenomenological 'feel' of 'in', 'with' and 'between' in human life. To get the full measure of what these 'mean' we need to replace their spatial connotation by a temporal one. That is to say our very prepositional uses have a metaphorical flavour about them. This intimation was already there in German idealist philosophy and among those influenced by it. Ideas are not 'in' the mind in the way biscuits are in a tin. But what other word can we use? Words have to be taken as pointers. As man is addressed by situation and circumstance, and more, by Being, Heidegger would say, his mode of response, in language, tends to be necessarily indirect. We are not now speaking of reference but of something more nuanced, of modes of expression which have to be seen through rather than grasped, of intuitions which can be communicated and shared, but shared obliquely. The metaphor needed is not the index finger of ostensive definition, but of entry into a region where light gradually dawns, where meanings nucleate around a core, fan out from a centre; where ripples from various centres meet, in turn setting up new centres of movement and so on without end.

This brings us to Heidegger's metaphors. A link leading to this third pointer is provided by the previous two pointers. Heidegger is passionately concerned with the Be-weg-ung of thought. Thought moves. But what is the whence and whither of thought? Philosophical thought is above all sent on its way by the question. To *experience* the question is already to be on the move, to be "an Weg". To question is not to be content with where one is. This can be illustrated well by a set of questions beginning with "why" directed on evil, injustice, betrayal and, incidentally, many matters on which at a personal level, Heidegger was peculiarly silent. It is a point which distinguishes philosophy from poetry, for poets do not as such deal in questions and answers. And yet the great poem can raise fundamental questions and the very texture of poetic discourse *can* embody the wisest of 'answers', given our finite human condition.

Attention was drawn just now to the incapsulation of the word 'Weg' in the verbal noun 'Bewegung'. For Heidegger, the path is more important than the goal. In a sense this means he is not interested in conclusions, in answers. There are a host of expressions he uses which incorporate the journey idea, e.g. 'Holzwege', 'Wegmarken', 'Unterwegs zur Sprache', 'Feldweg' and so on. Now the pilgrim idea is a familiar one in the western tradition. It always suggested linearity and was tied up with eschatology. But the way, for

Heidegger does not take us climbing onwards and upwards, and it leads neither to Plato's Form of the Good nor to Zion. It leads to a clearing in the woods where light can penetrate but where, when night overtakes us, we are surrounded by darkness. The image recalls the folklore of the Grimm brothers, the primeval forests of mythology. Each man draws his metaphors from his own experience and Heidegger belongs to the Black Forest and not the dappled woodlands of Vallombrosa or Aryavarta.

The etymological and metaphoric approaches fuse again in Heidegger's understanding of the meaning of *logos*. From the idea "to lay together" he proceeds to gathering and from this to emergence into non-concealment, and from here to utterance. His idea is that the essence of language is not in meaning but in the identity between uttering-in-language and letting-be-manifest. Could one say that the strategy is a replacement of 'mean' by 'can mean'? There is no doubt that the richness of terms used in philosophical discourse are susceptible of multiple interpretations. But to plumb *logos* or rather, for Heidegger, to respond to Being-as-utterance, is not to wander around amidst the more obvious meanings of words. We need to go beyond the said to the unsaid. The route is, as it were, from the within to the beyond. Heidegger speaks first in terms of the interrogation of Being, and this is elucidated through several metaphors, the act of surrender, letting-oneself-in-upon it, opening oneself, setting oneself upon the way of thought. We shall return to the 'opening' idea shortly.

Not all Heidegger's metaphors are strikingly new. To speak of Being as Light, as Source, is in consonance with the mainstream of the western metaphysical tradition. But to think of man as the 'lighting-up' of Being is to use language inventively and in a way which gives a very crucial status to finite being. For Being to greet, to hail, to beckon, is by implication, and in the words of a very different tradition (but one in which Heidegger was deeply interested), to work into *nirguna Brahman* some of the appeal of *saguna Brahman*. A metaphor is expanded into a myth in the fifth edition of *Was ist Metaphysik* (1949) when Heidegger employs a most primeval image, that of the tree. Metaphysics, he writes, is the root of the philosophy tree, and Being is the ground in which the roots are sunk.

The early metaphor of interrogation gradually gives way to that of 'listening' in Heidegger's thought, a shift that is very congruent with the stress on temporality that runs through his work. Coleridge had written of "the despotism of the eye"[30] and Heidegger is no less anxious to break out of the net of traditional concepts connected with vision. As in the case of the major shift in Wittgenstein's thinking,[31] the transition for Heidegger is expressed through a new metaphor. To attend is both to wait and to listen. To listen to *silence* is

---

[30]Vide *Biographia Literaria*, Ch. 6.
[31]Vide p. 64

none the less to listen. The sounds of the forest are often infinitesimal. To be attentive is to be ready to be addressed. That listening is to be understood metaphorically is clear from what we already know about Heidegger's way of philosophising. The natural object, the art object, the apparently 'dead' etymological root, *speak* to us. Heidegger could have found in music further ways of illustrating what he wanted to say, for music paradigmatically, 'gathers together', and 'opens up', and is to be listened to. Music is to be 'guarded' too when we exclude extraneous sounds, perform as excellently as we can, interpret the score as faithfully as possible. It is a dimension we are 'in' and thereby carried 'beyond', if we are music lovers. But Heidegger was more responsive to poetry and to painting than to music, and so the experience of listening comes to him mainly from his experience of forest life and from the written word.

Before examining his dialogue with the poets there are two pointers which remain for comment. Entering into a dialogue with one's predecessors is for Heidegger an indispensable form of listening for the philosopher, an indispensable way of sending thinking on its way. In sharp contrast to a great many linguistic analytic philosophers who think that the history of philosophy can be written off as a record of the follies of mankind, Heidegger is very conscious that the philosopher, and especially the metaphysician, is a participant in an on-going conversation whose many voices command attention. His method, and here he is like Jaspers, is to make the reader, the fellow-seeker, very conscious of a great tradition. He does not tilt swords, refute by means of argument. He indicates a new way. But we come across etymology again, for to engage in this cross-generation dialogue is to be made aware how words and expressions *have been* used. It is in this sense that language has to be *listened* to before one speaks or says something new. Such listening provides a path out of both prison-houses, the banality of the everyday and the strait-jackets of metaphysical systems.

The last pointer, the use of paradox[32], is an important one in defining Heidegger's relation to Hegel and to Kierkegaard. Heidegger's reaction to antinomies is more like Kierkegaard's than like Hegel's. Contradiction is not made a springboard to sublation. Opposites *belong* together in the paradox. They are not something which cries out for a logical solution. Whatever language we may use about Being inevitably has this character; inevitable not because this is the price paid for mis-employing categories, tearing down boundaries, going beyond experience, but because *our very experience* is witness to both features of the paradox. In the richest saying, speaking, we find both the said and the unsaid. The *logos* is both concealed and unconcealed. We undergo sometimes, in one and the same experience, the luminous, and the dark night of the soul. And it is the poets, even more than Kierkegaard that encourage Heidegger to believe that herein lies the profoundest truth.

[32] Vide Heidegger's *The Origin of the work of art* for many examples of paradoxical language.

Early in his career Heidegger had the insight that both thinker and poet are near to Being, that Pindar, Sophocles and Homer speak to us as authoritatively as Parmenides, Heraclitus and Plato, and that they are able to do this because they *respond* to the summons of Being. In later years he became a deep admirer of Hölderlin and Rilke and incorporated some of their language into his own thinking, yet he continued to ponder over the *difference* between philosophy and poetry, for difference there surely must be. In this connection, he is perhaps unique among philosophers in making particular poems the topic of philosophical lectures. In two Hölderlin interpretations ("Homecoming" and "Re-collection") in 1943 he speaks of the poet as a wanderer returning home, and it is from Hölderlin that he takes the idea of a fourfold relation between gods, mortals, earth and sky. The lecture entitled "Dichterisch wohnet der Mensch" delivered in October 1951 borrows its title from a line of Hölderlin's poem "In lieblicher Blaüe...." This poem chimes in with Heidegger's own interest in the "between". Man is between heaven and earth (cf. the symbolism of the Japanese art of 'Ikebana'); the poet is between man and the gods. The idea of dwelling, moreover, is a most fundamental one for Heidegger, and he develops it in several of his writings. The 1947 important statement *Brief über den Humanismus* contains many of Heidegger's best known elucidations of the human condition. Man is the lighting up of Being, the shepherd of Being. Language is the house of Being, and man dwells in this house. This means that he has privileged access to Being. But we are also told (the Holderlin essays) that the poet too 'dwells' in nearness to the source. In *Vorträge und Aufsätze* (1954) the meaning of 'dwelling' is further spelt out. The Gothic 'wunian', Heidegger tells us, from which 'wohnen' (to dwell) is derived, suggests tending, so "... the fundamental characteristic of dwelling is this (function of) tending..."[33] Meditations on Rilke and on Trakl are no less fruitful of ideas for Heidegger. It is Rilke[34] who calls Being "the open", and finds in Being what draws all beings into a whole. This ties in with Heidegger's own thought about 'gathering' in the discussion of *logos* and *legein*. In Trakl's poetry he finds that luminosity of the particular which in a lyric acts as the focus of poetic expression. The poet is able to gather Being in a particular place, a bridge, a pitcher, a building with words, as Van Gogh is able to in his painting of a chair, or a pair of shoes.

As for the idea of openness, Heidegger thinks of man's own existence as an aperture on Being, since man is able to articulate Being, through words, and through presumably works of art in various media, but most of all (this seems to be the main 'message') through the work of the philosopher and the poet. It is the poets who encourage him (the word inspiration is not inappropriate here) to link up working, dwelling and thinking, and this by now includes poeticising.

[33]p. 149.
[34]Vide *Holzwege* (1950) for Heidegger's discussion of Rilke.

Heidegger's near-reverential stance towards language lends itself to an interpretation like the following. Man dwells poetically because of his closeness to Being. Man is not a fabricator but a builder. What he builds with words are a special space, a special time, through which Being speaks to us. Yet it is equally true to say that we can speak because Being first speaks *to us*. The building not made by hands, in terms of imagery, is very much like the Greek temple, open to the sky. Without this openness man would not be capable of growth, of saying, of creating more, that is, of making further responses to the call of Being. The Greek image, white and shining as it is, has to be put alongside the Gothic one, the clearing in the woods whereon light shines, from where the sky can be seen and dark trunks of pine trees take the place of the white Green pillars. How far should we take this imagery? The Greek temple lies in a ruined state, with few pillars standing. The forest has been cut down in order to make a clearing. The surrounding woods are not lovely, dark and deep so much as dense and frightening. To be open is to be vulnerable, to both what is within and what is without us.

We seem to come very close to what distinguishes the thinker and the poet, and yet Heidegger leaves us with the riddle unsolved. We are once more "In Ulm, um Ulm, und um Ulm herum". Poeticising and thinking are just "nicht das gleiche" (not the same).[35] The poet experiences the abyss preparatory to being at home in the clearing. Both philosopher and poet strive to rescue language from banality. Both venture, both open up worlds for us. They make things manifest. To disclose Being is to articulate Truth. From the nature of philosophy and poetry we can discern, looking back as it were, how Being *needs* man, for it is only through man that Being is 'voiced'. There is a strong Nietzschean echo here: "All being wants to become word." Uncovering (*aletheia*) and bringing together (*sumballein*) are seen in philosophic discourse no less than in the work of art. And are we not familiar with the convergence of the two even outside the domains of philosophy and poetry, wherever we experience the heightened meaning of the particular? A particular garment (say a uniform no longer worn), a crofter's empty cottage on the hillside, a bombed site covered with willow-herb, a dumping-ground for discarded cars, the carefully-tended garden – these are all matters of 'common' experience, where we experience not a mere particular, an ultimate which terminates enquiry, the limit of analysis, the 'given', but an aperture on something more, a gathering[36] which leads in infinite directions. It is in such sessions of silent thought that we truly speak of *wonder*, a mode of awareness which when tempered (I use a metaphor from piano-making) appropriately gives rise to metaphysics and to poetry. That a sense of the tragic is never very far from such experiences can

---

[35] *Vorträge und Aufsätze*, p. 193.

[36] In his later writings Heidegger speaks of gathering rather than synthesis, a much less 'logical' word. The overtones are by no means agglomerative. I believe gleaning, bringing together, harvesting, are closer to what he means.

be gleaned from the examples just given, even the last, where the sight of leaf and blossom leads the mind to the inevitability of decay and death.

How far has Heidegger helped us to understand the difference between philosophy and poetry? Philosophy is "in a plight" (and for Heidegger the plight is by no means voiced in the superficial criticisms of verificationists) in a way in which poetry perhaps is not. Heidegger reminds us of the similar task faced by thinker and poet in searching for "les mots justes". Both enable us to look at things in new ways. There is a kind of "alert obedience"[37] which guides both in their use of language. The metaphysician, like the poet, discovers the uncanny in the familiar. In uncovering that which sustains he enables us to listen afresh, to see the familiar with new eyes.

Heidegger's understanding of the poet's craft is shaped by the poets he is familiar with. This is only natural. What if we say that much of recent poetry shows no sense of the translucence of the particular, and seems on the contrary to glorify the banal? Some contemporary poems are written in a speech which is "full of gaps and full of lights, filled with absences and over-nourishing signs, without foresight or stability of intention".[38] Heidegger can take this in, sensitive as he is to the pull of negative discourse in metaphysical thinking, the return to silence. And most of all the radical incompleteness of his own work witnesses to the *hazards* that beset the philosopher. While I myself feel that Heidegger was handicapped in his understanding of poetry by his neglect of music, i.e. sound, there is so much that is insightful in what he says that it is as if the compliment paid by Coleridge to philosophers (the poet *needs* to be a thinker) were being returned, for there is an implicit suggestion in Heidegger's own drawing on the work of poets with whose work he was familiar, that the philosopher needs to learn from the poets. What this lesson may be we have to spell out for ourselves – to refuse to *skirmish* with words, to root what is said in experience, to be alive to the natural symbolism of the everyday, to possess a patience which thinks less in terms of *wresting* meanings through arguments than presenting insights in a form which is both intelligible and sensible, to be gifted with a piety of thinking which submits to the call of Being and articulates it as faithfully as one can. Put in this way it is not a lesson which the greatest philosophers failed to learn. But it is a lesson which the philosopher in the twentieth century may have to learn afresh.

---

[37] A phrase used by Heidegger in his *Principles of Thinking*, 1958.
[38] *Writing Degree Zero and Elements of Semiology*, Roland Barthes, Eng. Tr., p. 48.

CHAPTER VIII

The Myth of Description

So far our investigations have led in the following direction. The history of philosophy shows a dominant tendency to support a concept of reason kept free of the 'contaminating' influence of the non-rational. In the late eighteenth century, an opposite tendency appeared which recognised the subsoil out of which reason grows and which indeed feeds it. Even among those who sail under a rationalist banner it is possible to discern what I have called a linguistic imagination at work. This should not be hypostatised into a faculty. Rather it can be seen as a capacity philosophical thinking has for utilising its sensible experience in markedly non-inferential ways so as to throw light on the very texture that experience has. Linguistic imagination shows itself to be operative variously in philosophical discourse, including the choosing of examples[1] believed to 'show' a point, the designing of hypothetical cases, the constructing of models, the use of metaphor. Of these it was the last that was singled out for discussion. It was found that even though analytic philosophers (this abbreviated expression may be pardoned) lay much store by examples, hypothetical cases and models, they are also quite free in their use of metaphorical expressions, some of which throw considerable light on how they regard the philosophical enterprise. For example, it was noticed that a large number of words used by them indicated "something gone wrong" e.g. being dragged, held captive, being in a fly bottle, trap, cage, suffering cramps and the like. While these drew attention usefully to the way in which thinking can be held up, there was a tendency to neglect the many ways in which seminal expression can send thinking on its way. Certain strong linguistic preferences seemed to dictate which analogies are regarded as sinister and which beneficent. Freudian discoveries about the nature of conscious processes have encouraged the view in some quarters that our linguistic preferences are controlled by factors, potent indeed, of which we are not aware. This appears to reinforce the verificationist thesis that philosophical discourse is not a matter of truth and falsity. In the meantime it is not only those engaged in linguistic analysis who are interested in the language of philosophy, in fact their interest in philosophy *of* language has in large part, and ironically of

[1] *Vide* my paper "Two views of inductive philosophizing", *Kant-Studien*, Heft 3, 1967.

course, made them less than sensitive to it. Phenomenological interest in language stems from the belief that consciousness is intentional. The phenomenologist finds in speech something which is both grounded and directed. Heidegger is unique among those who, in the course of venturing to found a phenomenological ontology, discern much in common between the philosopher and the poet. No doubt he is thinking of the philosopher of a certain kind and the poet of a certain kind. Both philosopher and poet strive for an articulation of experience in a form of discourse which is par excellence not ordinary, not usual. There is a concentrated, *distilled* character about both philosophic and poetic discourse. The choice of words is in each case governed by a sense of *importance* which operates alongside a keen awareness of the common *habitus* of speech. When successful both philosopher and poet give the impression of having something to say and of saying it well.

But surely, it will be objected, the central thing about philosophical discourse, about the language of philosophy, is argument. We need here, it seems to me, to be on guard against over-simplifying the nature of argument in philosophy. Much progress has been made in this century in distinguishing between types of philosophical reasoning. Philosophical discourse embodies a number of strategies which are found to be philosophically profitable. The philosopher uncovers hidden premises, resolves contradictions, discovers links between different fields of philosophical enquiry. The labour of thought can enlist figures of myth (e.g. the Sun) and images which can assist its work. All this is possible because language encapsulates the history of thought, a thinking where initially distinctions of sensible and intelligible, cognition and contrivance, were not yet made. Both philosophy and poetry labour to unfold what is encapsulated, although this by no means exhausts their task. This is not a regressive procedure. The labour of fresh thinking is many-structured. The fuse of philosophical thinking is not always lit in the same way. It can be lit by the scholar's exploration of encapsulated etymological roots, by the intimation of complex meanings rippling out from a centre, by the teleological out-reach towards a challenging concept, by the profound insight of great literature, by the disquiet set in motion by the perception of similitude and dissimilitude. Once the fuse is lit, thinking goes on its way. We trail clouds of spatial analogies (the language of polarity and tendency), cosmic and political ones (harmony, the strife of opposites, the reconciliation of antitheses). We encounter the elusive and the enigmatic, the paradoxical and the ironic. Philosophical arguments are delicately filamented, and the relation of argument to insight cannot be elucidated in any simple manner. Lonergan speaks of "supposing, thinking, considering, formulating, defining" as occurring "in conjunction with" insights.[2] But the phrase "in conjunction with" expresses the matter all too loosely. The strategies we employ both mediate the insights we

---

[2] "Metaphysics as Horizon", *Gregorianum*, 1963) pp. 307-13.

have and are an expression of them. Much of philosophical argument is concerned not so much with settling a philosophical dispute as with clarifying an insight. Such insights require progressive articulation, an articulation sustained by actuality and continuously subject to self-criticism. It should also not be missed that an argument can be used to *suspend* argument – a technique sometimes used by Hume.

Now among the various strategies found philosophically profitable the philosophical metaphor is thought to be offensive by some since it supposedly offends against the "virtual seriality" of philosophical argument in providing a lens of meaning whose totality floods it and seems to free us from the obligation to trace whence we have come. We are not, however, thereby released from the obligation to provide a reasoned discourse any more than the traveller by air is debarred from going on foot over the territory he has seen in a flash and whose intricate topography indeed invites and tantalises. Linear discourse has been a paradigm for centuries. In this connection, Max Black has made an interesting remark: "Even at its most lucid, discourse is inescapably linear, doling out scraps of meaning in a fragile thread. But significant thought is seldom linear: cross references and overlapping relationships must be left for the good reader to tease out by himself."[3] Black says this in the context of the disparity between linear verbal form and non-linear conceptual structure both in mathematics and in literature. His point can be well illustrated in the ways we have found philosophers use language. A more or less linear strength comes to a knot, a sticky patch; implications come to a dead end or, alternatively, lead in too many directions, and we have to start on a different tack. The momentum of thought goes on, as the momentum of a theme does during a pause in music. The exposition is taken up through an example, a counter-example, or through worrying away, as it were, at a different part of the jigsaw puzzle.

But I would quarrel here with Black's polarization of discourse and significant thought. We can certainly speak of philosophical discourse and poetic discourse. When claim is made to *argument,* and (phenomenologists apart) the philosopher mostly makes this claim, claim is made to a certain sequentiality about the steps taken, a sequentiality which amounts to what Black calls 'discourse'. Now even when the philosopher argues, it is often found that he does this in a Pickwickian way. He may say "Stop arguing. Look!" Are we to say this is *part* of his argument, or is he abandoning argument in favour of a different strategy? Even without this peculiar case the situation is odd enough. The presentation of an example is a parallel strategy to the setting out of an argument. It is an interpolation which we are supposed to take as throwing light obliquely on the thrust of the argument. It is for this reason that Kant

[3] *The Labyrinth of Language,* Britannica Perspectives, Encyclopedia Britannica Inc., William Benton (Pub.), Volume 3, 1968, p. 20.

distrusted examples. Counter examples can upset the apple-cart. His own special kind of argument, the transcendental proof, needed no support from examples. My point is really this. Taking up the terms of discussion as given in the quotation from Black, philosophical discourse seems to be a peculiar *amalgam* of linear and non-linear structures. This can be illustrated as well from Wittgenstein's way of philosophising (which tends to be non-linear par excellence in his second and third phases as distinct from the *Tractatus* which is almost wholly linear) as from Heidegger's. The non-linearity is exhibited very clearly whenever metaphors occur (my own view is that 'examples', 'reminders' etc. also break linearity) which is why the use of metaphors in philosophical writing came in for scrutiny in our study. What bearing does this have on the understanding of a philosophical text, the hermeneutical problem? I venture to offer here a metaphor drawn from music.

The understanding of a philosophical text seems to me to be far more like listening to a fugue than looking at a landscape or a picture, or still less, trying to look at the landscape in the light of different pictures. We strive to follow the thread and contrapuntally to appreciate the harmonies. There is an ornament here, a pause there; and these must be savoured. Who would say that this inverted mordent was dispensable? It bears a subtle relation to the texture of the whole work. Take a passage somewhere in the middle of a Bach Three-Part Invention. It trails clouds of implication backwards and forwards, upwards and downwards. But it is on the move. The final chord is not like a conclusion. But the vocal lines are tied up, and rounded off in a certain way. The philosophical text is much more like this than it is like a page of symbols in a text-book of symbolic logic. It has a logic of its own. And there is something more. In working on a philosophical text, in trying to understand it, a certain refraction takes place, and this depends on the language itself and on who, where and how the reader is. This refraction can be felt in Aquinas' understanding of Aristotle, Hegel's of Kant, and Heidegger's of Kierkegaard, to take a few examples. It is because of the plenitude of the text (and I am thinking here of the great philosophical text, although this certainly raises other questions) that this refraction is made possible. It is a refraction, which no doubt accommodates 'faithful' interpretations no less than misunderstandings, and perhaps a range of interpretations in between.

Let us think of the variety of responses that we make to a philosophical text, including our response to a part of it, be it a chapter, a sequence of thought or an argument (the line has been taken in preceding discussions that while not every sequence of philosophic thought *constitutes* an argument, some of such sequences play an important, and some an indispensible *role* in argument). Let us assume that the first thing needed is to understand what is being said, and that this involves not only what is textual but what is contextual. Not all such contextual material can be deemed presuppositional, but certainly some of it can. Then how do we react next? We use words like interesting, ingenious, wrong-headed, tortuous, involved, seductive, misleading, sound. We may be 'convinced', or we may existentially appropriate the *Weltanschauung* presented, or we may regard the whole fabric as a tissue of fairy tales, as inadequate, inappropriate and so on. Even those philosophical viewpoints which purport to be existentially neutral, and purport to avoid ontological commitment, arouse great partisanship, and other ways of doing philosophy are dubbed out of date, wrong-headed, misleading etc. Even those who regard philosophy as unconcerned with truth and falsity show by their choice of epithets that they regard their own way of philosophising to be the correct one and all other alternatives to be incorrect. One would have thought that if all philosophisings were dubbed exercises in illusion-spinning this would apply no less to the exercise issuing in this particular point of view. This can hardly be got round by a recourse to levels of statements, first order, second order and the like, although this is usually the gambit chosen by those who claim exemption for their own particular view.

Now if we look at the great variety of epithets we use in our response to a philosophical text or segment of it, we notice that we do not have occasion to react in such ways to sequences of mathematical inference, or scientific theorizing. The epithets are altogether more like the language we use in response to a work of art. Strong feelings are aroused when anything new comes along, schools of opinion align themselves, critics sharpen their pencils and great controversy is aroused. The Freudians and Marxists both have their explanations ready; in the one case deep feelings are said to be aroused because of the unconscious desires etc. triggered off; and in the other, because any social phenomenon reflects the relation between the forces of production and the tensions brought about by the relative balance of the forces in any particular period.

But if we liken the philosophical text to a work of art, do we not abandon all too easily the traditional metaphysical concern with truth? The problem of truth has in fact been dogging us all along, and here is the crunch, critics will say. The variety of ways in which the genesis of philosophical questions comes about was noticed earlier. This in no way casts a reflection on the importance of such questions. But what determines our decision that a particular answer 'fits' a particular question? No doubt one way of beginning to deal with all this is to eliminate bogus questions, those depending purely on grammar and so on. Even about these there can of course be endless controversy. Moreover, the cues given by grammar should not be regarded as necessarily misleading. We saw, for example, how Heidegger drew valuable insights about our various 'dispositions' from prepositions. But what about the remaining questions? Does the dichotomy, question/answer, perhaps itself mislead, as dichotomies in philosophy often do? Does not, say, one question rather lead to *another*? In that case one would never arrive at the consideration of 'fit'. But this seems too extreme an alternative. Let us grant that there are genuine philosophical questions and putative answers to them. What answers we accept as satisfactory seem to be closely connected with what we regard as ultimate, and people can certainly differ a very great deal as to what they regard as ultimate. The decision to terminate questioning and regard a particular matter as 'settled' is a very individual matter. To take an example, to one man the 'answer' given to the problem of evil in the closing chapters of the Book of Job is an ultimate one. To another, it is no answer at all.

But, it will be objected, we are still far from coming to grips with truth. We need to retrace our steps a little, before we can proceed further with this. The investigation of the language of philosophy shows evidence of a *striving for expression* which links the philosopher with workers in other branches of the humanities. His work does not stand or fall through sheer comparison with the facts any move than a portrait is deemed excellent on account of any simple style correspondence it may appear to have with the original. My choice of the analogy of the portrait is deliberate as talk of "using pictures", is still fashionable in analytical circles, as if we were faced with a choice of lenses among which we could opt according to our temperament. If we are to choose analogies from the visual arts let us do so in less crude a manner. Photography, which began as the most 'representative' of the arts, has moved a long way in recent decades. The contemporary photographer who uses a 'soft focus' does so in the service of a radically individual perspective which throws up in a vivid manner "just how things are". The blurred edges, the apparently distorted vision, is precisely what makes the experience of looking at the photograph more than a purely visual one. We feel that we ourselves are sitting on the park with the tramp; we know how he feels; the leafless trees mirror his condition and ours. How far we are from both the language of correspondence and the heuristic stances of 'seeing-as'! We experience intimations of an ontological rooting which reverberates in our own very being. Part of this is captured in the phrase "true to life" which we use with reference to the great novel, the avant-garde photograph. The perception of what is "true-to" is a response to the sense of an actuality which *sustains* rather than *constrains*. It is, it seems to me, precisely this sense of a sustaining actuality which we have in the face of a metaphysical work to which we are attuned. How much of this "tuning" can be attributed to temperament? That the idealist and the realist differ in temperament is a commonplace. What causes a gritting of the teeth in one chimes in with the verdict of individual insight in another. The languages used by each is finely honed in keeping with an overall style, a characteristic idiom of thought. The tender-minded (in James' phrase) philosopher is likely to explore 'soft focus', to find in surface textures not an occasion for being *constrained* but a cue for further probing. Such a thinker will be sensitive to the multiple resonances of language, to the resources that language has. We referred to this capacity earlier as that of linguistic imagination. It was found at work in thinkers as diverse as Husserl, Waismann and

Heidegger. Linguistic imagination tends to issue in metaphysical thinking (although we also found it put in the service of an anti-metaphysical impulse as in, say, the writings of Ryle) because it hinges on the perception of similitude and dissimilitude which occasions transfers of vocabulary – and this in turn is founded on that same sensitivity to quiddity which engenders an ontology.

From the analogy of photography I wish to move to analogies from two other spheres, one of which concerns language directly, that is, translation,[4] the second being derived from the performative arts. Both of these are spheres where the language of 'true-to' may perhaps be found applicable. The difficulty of translating from one language to another is a familiar one. To translate from language A to language B I must have a sufficient knowledge of both languages. It is not open to the conscientious translator to be selective. He should not say, "This particular overtone I cannot catch, so I will leave it out." If the translator is called upon to be conscientious in this respect, so also is the metaphysician. The latter cannot (should not) say, "Unfortunately consideration X does not fit my theory, so I will leave it out." In translating, and this is interesting, we progressively *approximate* to the meaning. Translation X is not bad, Y is somewhat better, but even here something has been left out. As for translation Z, this seems closest to what is meant. Sometimes we apologise at this stage and say, "Of course this phrase cannot really be translated. You must read the original for yourself." In other cases, we are completely satisfied, as when we agree that "Here is my aunt's pen" can be adequately translated into "Voici la plume de ma tante". Here one sentence "corresponds to the other". When we are dealing with matters difficult to translate it may be said to be the business of the translator to "bring us to the point where we see". The translator's efforts do not result in any sensible experience gained by ourselves, but in an advance in understanding, in insight. You cannot *verify* if a translation is or is not satisfactory. A translation can be good or bad, correct or incorrect, but not true or false.

Let us look at a few more difficulties which attend the task of translation. Say the translator decides something cannot be translated. One way out is for him to incorporate it as it is into his translation. Similarly a philosopher may incorporate something recalcitrant into his theory, something which is bound to remain unassimilated and which gives an easy foothold for the critic (compare say the difficulty neutral monists have with after-images, memories and the like). The translator also faces the problem of packed-in meanings and associations. For example, the word Kant uses for 'leading-strings' is linked up with the German for pulling someone by the nose, an overtone which is absent from the English expression. The translator must concern himself as much with what is suggested as with what is stated, and this is why translating poetry is so

---

[4] The argument at this point is partly drawn from my contribution on "The Meaning of Metaphysics" at a seminar at the University of Madras in October 1967 and printed in the Proceedings of the same.

notoriously difficult. Is translation completely intra-linguistic? Probably not. The translator needs to bring to bear upon his task something more than the word to word approach. The outcome is that he is able to say 'This is what is meant' although he is able, one might say, to give no more than circumstantial evidence for his judgement. The poor translator is the piecemeal one, i.e. the literal one. Yet no doubt there are occasions when the literal approach may be the best or the only approach possible cf. in simultaneous interpreting at the diplomatic level. The translator encounters something analogous to both the constraining and sustaining influence of actuality referred to a little while ago. He is constrained by his knowledge of what is meant, and he is sustained by his total familiarity with the languages in question and the forms of life they are associated with. He is often guided in the exclusion of a certain putative translation by the thought of "what cannot be said".

Many philosophical problems to do with meaning, communication, the understanding of 'difficult' language, have been raised in recent discussions about translation, particularly in the context of the structuralist thesis about language. My own concern is far more limited. First of all, I find an analogy between the "intra-linguistic cum extra-linguistic" involvement of the translator and the metaphysician. The translator is apparently concerned with a purely intra-linguistic affair, finding equivalent, (or as near-equivalent as he can) expressions. In so doing, however, he works in a plenum, his knowledge of what it is like to be a German-speaking, French-speaking individual and of total environments and idioms that this involves. In a sense this is the extra-linguistic element, and in another it is as thoroughly linguistic as it could be. The intra-linguistic concourse in which the metaphysician participates is one in which his predecessors and his contemporaries are co-participants. As Heidegger and Jaspers have stressed, to philosophise is to perform something which has a historical dimension. Even those who take pride in ignoring the history of philosophy (they seem to be confined to this century) cannot avoid an implict dialogue with thinkers of the past.

Secondly, the experience of careful refining of expression is common to both the translator and the metaphysician. The words are not quite the ones we want. There is a conscious striving which is never fully satisfied. A curious but unmistakeable integrity directs this search for a more 'faithful' form of expression. The question is not merely that of precision. To this extent both translator and metaphysician are seized with a passion for verity, for verisimilitude. It can be seen why I have now shifted from talk of the philosopher to that of the metaphysician. There are obviously technical reaches in philosophy especially concerning the logic of implication, where other kinds of linguistic skill are called into play. But the metaphysician must needs be involved with verity to the extent of obsessive concern. No metaphysician in the past has been a mere system builder. Each was impelled by a passion to articulate a vision of that which *sustains* (the word Being here is the most appropriate one), an environing whose gradual articulation involved both the awareness of constraint and the awareness of possibility. The characteristic caution which the good translator exercises has an affinity with the caution we need to exercise in philosophical discourse. The work of the translator, familiar and everyday as it is, gives us an analogue of the metaphysician's activity in several respects. But just as in these times the translator's art receives scant recognition, the metaphysician's labours only too often tend to fare likewise.

The third analogy, from the performative arts, is as follows. Consider three performances of a particular string quartet, first on Hi-Fi, then on an ordinary record, and then as played live by an amateur ensemble. Or consider the character of Hamlet as played by Burbage and by Gielgud. Let us contrast these two with our second analogy. In the case of translation we can say, "The original is in English. (Say, a play by Shakespeare). It has been translated into 60 other languages." In the third analogy can we raise the question of an original at all? In the case of translation the question of correspondence does not always arise, for although some words correspond to each other (e.g. cat = chat) and in learning a new language we begin with such simple correspondences, many *sentences* may not properly do so because of the idiosyncrasies of syntactical structure, idiom, and what, for the want of a better term, can be called the 'genius' of the languages concerned. In the third analogy, the question of correspondence does not arise because the original is itself a construction. What is a drama or a musical work unplayed? An organization of symbols on paper (cf. the complicated structure of this with the problem of a table unperceived. A table is a perceivable object but not a symbol. The musical score is a perceivable object and also a system of symbols which is to be 'read'.) Can we here speak of approximating to something? But approximating to what? Is a costume performance of 'Hamlet' on an apron stage more authentic than one in modern dress? If an actress over forty years of age plays Juliet, has the dramatist's intention been done violence to? We usually think that baroque works played on the instruments of the period concerned have a special authenticity, even though the entire technology of modern acoustics and sophisticated amplifying devices may have to be employed so that the sound can fill the concert hall. The play, the musical score, are texts which have to be interpreted, performed and understood, before they can be responded to by an audience. Where is this analogy leading us?

There were centuries when the metaphor of the divine signature was a very familiar one used by religious thinkers, the choir of heaven and earth being regarded as a 'text' whose divine authorship could be discerned by the believer. A secularised version of this sees the universe as replete with meanings revealed as it were at the nodal points where sensible cue and experience meet. The idea of cue is there in all the analogies we have used so far, the scene photographed, the text to be translated, the text or score to be performed. In each case the quiddity of the work is more than the cue, is in fact the total symbolic structure we call the work of art. And there is an openness about this very structure which makes it hospitable, in our examples, to different prints, new translations, different types of production, further styles of performance. And amidst all these variants there is an approximating, an openness which invites greater depth of understanding. In this approximative process we are guided by a judgement which is able to adjudicate between the better and the worse, the more and less successful. The metaphysician, too, is guided by an alert obedience which leads him to sharpen his ideas, improve upon his expressions. He who reads the text, like the man who watches the play or listens to the symphony, brings to bear upon his understanding of the text the new resources of contemporary scholarship which may enlighten or distort just as new fashions or recent technological apparati in the performative arts may be thought by critics to have an improving or distorting effect. We are in each case in a field where there is a strange conflation of discursive and intuitive capacities at work e.g. a following of the narrative of event along with an insight into character (say, in responding to *Hamlet*), a following of argument along with a pari passu critical insight into its flaws. The photographer is not merely recording; the translator is not describing, he is aiming at more than literality; the concert artiste is also not describing, he interprets a score, and the more authoritative the rendering, paradoxically the more latitude in terms of tempi and volume is considered justifiable by knowledgeable critics. In each case we speak of 'true-to' where this has the varying shades of meaning of true to life (the photo), a faithful rendering (the translation), an authentic performance (the drama or musical work). In each case, moreover, the negatively graded versions (we cannot speak here of the *converse*) have nothing to do with falsity. Take each example. A photo may be 'poor', a translation 'not good enough', a dramatic or musical performance "a travesty", "not up to the mark" and so on. So there are domains of our common experience where we recognise the shock of truth, of authenticity, without being bullied into accepting the view that truth and falsity are necessarily dichotomous expressions. Furthermore, the empirical anchorages which the language of philosophy may seem to need in order to save it from the charge of spinning illusion cannot be simply *appealed* to any more than we can appeal to a section of landscape, the text, the original, in the task of assessing involved in our three analogies. The relation of the language of philosophy to what it is 'about' is even more subtle than the relation of a translation to its original or a performance of a play or musical work to the system of symbols in which it is written. It was necessary to point out that we are all familiar with fields where, as a matter of ordinary usage, it is perfectly in order to speak of being true to life, of being a faithful rendering, of being the authentic Bach, Shakespeare or whatever. The criteria in such examples are not provided by looking on 'fact' as a terminus of enquiry, but by skilled interpretation of the data in accordance with standards of evaluation proper to each field. The scope of the analogies is obviously limited and I should not want to press them further than as indicated.

All this, it may be objected, has some relevance to philosophers who do 'revisionary' metaphysics, but none at all to those who follow a 'descriptive' programme. As the whole distinction between 'revisionary' and 'descriptive' metaphysics is quite untenable given the kind of phenomenology of the language of philosophy followed through in the preceding chapters we must attend to this objection in some detail.

Anyone familiar with both philosophical and non-philosophical writing cannot help being struck by the peculiar use contemporary philosophers make of the word 'description'. The literary mind sees description as polar not to speculation but to digression. As Locke was perhaps the first philosopher to inaugurate the fashion of philosophical description with his "historical, plain method" it is interesting to note the combination of admiration and irony with which Sterne speaks of the *Essay*. Tristram, the narrator of *Tristram Shandy* says: "...I will tell you in three words what the book is – It is a history – A history! of who? what? where? when? Don't hurry yourself. It is a history-book, Sir (which may possibly recommended it to the world) of what passes in a man's own mind...."[5] In the context of fiction, description means narrative: in the context of historical writing, description is taken as polar to discussion: and in day to day conversation to describe is usually to give information. The non-philosopher may indeed be most surprised to learn that philosophers describe at all, still more, to hear that this is considered by some to be the most respectable thing for philosophers to do. In ordinary life we know what it is like to improve upon a description, make it more precise, vivid, detailed etc. All descriptions are partial, and some are 'thin'. Experience of the non-adequation of description to event is familiar to those on both sides of the bench in a court of law. What is disclosed is often so done through the *gaps* in narration. We may, for reasons of our own, make our descriptions deliberately obscure, as in the cryptic descriptions of hidden treasure, or in the guarded statements made under interrogation. To describe is, in any case, not at all like hitting a target. We can describe events in the past and present, we can describe imaginary situations, and we can use imagination in describing actual situations. We have some idea, then, of what the uses of the word 'description' are in ordinary language. The philosopher's use of the word 'description' does not seem to come from ordinary usage, and as this may be the unkindest cut of all, we must examine how this has come about.

It was largely impatience with definitions and with theorising that turned a number of philosophers, from Moore to Austin, towards description. Moore's Butlerian dictum "Everything is what it is and not another thing" encouraged a

---

[5] *The Life and Opinions of Tristram Shandy, Gentleman.* Vol. II, Ch. ii, in the edn. of J.A. Work, New York, 1940, p. 85.

simplified view of description which left out the consideration that there are *resemblances* between things on the basis of which transfers of vocabulary are highly meaningful. Sometimes language points like an arrow, but at other times it has the roundaboutness of a natural gesture. Moore apart, Wittgenstein bears his share of responsibility for the fashionable interest in description shown by analytic philosophers. The *Tractatus* puts forward description as depiction, stressing the matching role of language in a situation where facts are arranged in a determinate way, and talk about them arranged likewise. The *Tractatus'* distinction between saying (where saying means describing) and showing was later modified by recognising different ways of saying, some of which are not describing at all. But in spite of this later recognition of the complexity of language, or because of it, the in-thing for the philosopher to do became *describing* the various uses of language. This way one could avoid ontological commitment, something deemed to be desirable. Smuggled in, of course, was an ontological commitment to the alleged rock-bottom character of the commonplace. The use of the word 'description' became increasingly Pickwickian. Descriptive discourse is towards 'the outside' according to our most common usage. The doctor is more likely to say "Tell me how you feel" rather than "Describe how you feel." The medical student at an examination, however, may be required to "Describe the symptoms etc. of disease X". Descriptive discourse is suitable neither for elucidating the inner, nor for a mode of philosophising which disallows the distinction between inner and outer. However, those who did their would-be philosophical describing well were awarded encomiums by confrères working on the same lines. Urmson and Warnock refer to Austin's " 'truthfulness and accuracy' in the use, and in description of the use of words and phrases",[6] which, incidentally, incorporates an intriguing use of the word 'truthful'. A very salutary warning, however, was given by Gilbert Ryle. He speaks of the "....smothering effect of using notions like depicting, describing, explaining, and others to cover highly disparate things...."[7] One can see why this caveat is given by Ryle rather than by anyone else. Ryle's forte is the plotting of criss-cross similarities, intersecting and overlapping concepts, and these can be drawn attention to rather than described. Nor were those who wanted to press home the distinction between surface grammar and depth grammar very successful in their appropriation of the language of description, for 'uncovering' is not very like describing. Not much grist for the 'descriptive mill' can be derived from talk of models either, for models do not describe directly; a model *enables* description without being itself descriptive. Then again a good deal of philosophical argument is devoted to adjudicating between good and bad reasoning, and this too, surely is not to describe.

[6]"J.L. Austin", in *Mind* (1961), reprinted in *The Linguistic Turn*, ed. by Richard Rorty, pp. 248-9.
[7]*Dilemmas*, p. 81.

In spite of all these disadvantages weighed against the use of the word 'description' by philosophers, the use received a boost from a new direction when Strawson formulated what seemed at first sight to be an illuminating distinction between descriptive and revisionary metaphysics. Speculative metaphysics, so the theory goes, proposes a scheme about things as they 'really' are, and does this through revising our actual conceptual scheme. Through the revised conceptual scheme we were not going to "see things differently; it is presented as a picture of things as they really are, instead of as they delusively seem. And this presentation, with its contrast between esoteric reality and daily delusion, involves and is the consequence of the unconscious distortion of ordinary concepts, i.e. of the ordinary use of linguistic expression."[8] The first sentence is rather puzzling, for presenting things as they really are is presumably a recommendation to see things differently. However, the distinction between 'descriptive' and 'revisionary' is made far more clearly in *Individuals,* as follows:,"...descriptive metaphysics is content to describe the actual structure of thought about the world, revisionary metaphysics is concerned to produce a better structure."[9] The distinction has been the centre of extensive discussion in the journals, and it would not have concerned us here at all were it not for the fact that it seems to perpetuate precisely the same over-simplified view of the language of philosophy that it has been the main purpose of this study to criticise. The most debatable pronouncement occurs early on in Strawson's book: "There is a massive central core of human thinking which has no history – or none recorded in histories of thought; there are categories and concepts which, in their most fundamental character, change not at all."[10] And yet at the same time the author grants that "certainly concepts do change, and not only, though mainly, on the specialist periphery; and even specialist changes react on ordinary thinking".[11] Now we cannot have it both ways. Either there is a central core or there is not. Whatever candidates for the central core there may be, say the concepts of substance, space and time, causality and perhaps a few others, they have changed radically over the years. Apart from changes in concepts, there is also the very important factor of *refinement* of concepts, a process that goes on at all the levels we can think of, the everyday, the scientific and the philosophical. There is a great deal of give and take between the changes and refinements that go on among the different language strata pertinent to the various disciplines. The more sophisticated the thinking, the greater is the evidence of transfers and borrowings. The would-be metaphysician in his search for a world-be a-historical core seems to be

---

[8]"Analysis, Science and Metaphysics" in *The Linguistic Turn,* ed. by R. Rorty, University of Chicago Press. The paper was originally presented in the Royaumont Colloquium of 1961, i.e. two years after the publication of *Individuals.*
[9]*Individuals,* p. 9.
[10]*Ibid.* p. 10.
[11]*Ibid.* p. 10.

misguided. He is misguided not only in his disregard of the kind of changes noted by Collingwood, but in his disregard of the linguistic plurality drawn attention to by Whorf and others. If we need to do over again in each age the work of descriptive metaphysics (as Strawson grants) this shows that there *is* no a-historical core. Moreover, the programme of the descriptive metaphysician is queerly named, for what he is reckoned to do is to expose and take note, and this is surely more like analysing than describing. Furthermore, if the alleged rock-bottom framework which is the topic of his description is as basic as all that, it can hardly be *described,* because it itself will be the *condition* of description. It is for this reason that, while Locke's methodology seems to fall midway between criticism and description, Kant's is out and out critical and not descriptive at all.

Those who advocate descriptive metaphysics tend to polarise the possibilities of seeing things aright and seeing things delusively, a polarisation which is itself a distortion of the state of affairs. Let us think of the great variety of examples that can be given of "seeing things differently". There are constant shifts in the focus of our understanding which take place from day to day. The man with equal fluency in two very different languages, especially where the culture patterns are very different as well, knows how different things can seem in each of the two life-worlds between which he has learned to commute comfortably. The person who successfully undergoes a course of psychiatric therapy learns to see his whole situation differently, an insight which may come, not in the Gestalt manner, in a flash, as in the case of alternating perceptions of an ambiguous figure, but through the painstaking appraisal of all the factors at work in his existential predicament. Fatigue, elation, absent-mindedness – all these make us 'see differently'. To "see differently" is not, ipso facto, to see either correctly or incorrectly. The analytic philosopher is, in fact, let down by his oracle of "ordinary experience" and "ordinary use". To deliberate on the structure of human thought (another way in which the descriptive metaphysician speaks of the in-thing to do) is to engage in what I can only refer to as a highly involuted activity, a reflective operation where we are consciously hoisting ourselves by our own bootstraps. The pendulum swings between familiar and unfamiliar uses of expressions is radically misunderstood if it is polarised into the divide between correct and incorrect. It is not paraphrase which can clarify what lies embedded in our language. Our 'unformalised' linguistic expressions are elusive rather than deceptive. We do not succeed when we impale them on the butterfly-collector's pins of particularity, for particularity no less than description, in the sense in which philosophers use these terms, is a myth. What the descriptive metaphysician honours with the name of 'particulars' are loosely textured clusters, cues for multiple interpretations. The distinction between surface and depth, the overt and the submerged, has point in so far as it indicates complexity, but it is systematically misleading (to return the compliment) if only the submerged is regarded as "being what is the case". The thatness which sets human activity in motion, is not a terminus but an index of possibility, a take-off point for scientific investigation no less than for artistic creation, and also for explorations usually deemed purely intellective, such as philosophising. We do not gain guidance in our exploratory thinking, whether this be the distilled discourse of the poet, or the 'reasoned' discourse of the philosopher, by constantly reminding ourselves of the commonplace. The main reason why I regard philosophical description as a myth is that it is an extremely *inadequate* way of referring to the very complex activities we have been investigating in discussing the language of philosophy.

It may be objected that not only analysts but phenomenologists too regard their activities as descriptive. The former purport to describe uses of language and the latter purport to describe essences. There are interesting parallels. The analyst wishes to be free from "misleading analogies", and the phenomenologist wishes to be free from presuppositions, as Husserl puts it, from the "mania peculiar to modern life, to theorize everything".[12] Both, claiming Frege as a father figure, are wary about the dictates of grammar. The analyst's manifesto about unveiling basic categories is matched by the phenomenologist's manifesto about reduction, which, likewise, is aimed at enabling us to reach a stratum not otherwise get-at-able. The division of opinion with respect to naturalism should not be missed. The phenomenologist shuns naturalism like the plague. The linguistic analyst, with his faith in the oracle of the market-place, is a naturalist in his own right, and therefore not sensitive to infection. Now the phenomenologist speaks of his work as "descriptive" not out of any affection for the word but in order to set the record straight. Talk about the immanent contents of consciousness, suspiciously idealist though it may sound, is nothing of the kind. We are talking about something objective after all. The word "elucidation" used by some of the French phenomenologists indicates rather more happily what the phenomenological way of doing philosophy is like. We elucidate structures of consciousness rather than describe them. The phenomenologist's programme does not *hinge* on the idea of description. But the analyst's idiom of philosophising does.

---

[12] *The Crisis of European Sciences and Transcendental Phenomenology*, Edmund Husserl, Trans, David Carr. Northwestern University Press, Evanston, 1970, p. 131.

CHAPTER IX

Epilogue

The Ariadne's thread to be grasped in these labyrinthine chapters can be put in the form of a question: What light does a study of the language of philosophy throw on the whole enterprise of philosophising, and, as a result of this study, are we any nearer penetrating what might be called, not too fancifully, the aspiration of reason? There can obviously be no simple answer to a question of this kind. The advice the Boyg gives Peer Gynt, "to go round about", is advice we cannot help following. Language is not so much a tool as a resource. Those who write *well,* whether they be philosophers or no, explore these resources in a way which goes beyond the 'ordinary'. Skilful writing calls into play an unstated hinterland, a range of the unsaid. As Gadamer puts it, finite human discourse "brings into play a totality of meaning without being able to say it totally".[1] This is to acknowledge that semantic discourse is fed from both semantic and non-semantic sources.

Does it help at this stage to speak of the philosopher, no less than, say, the poet, as a 'creative' writer? The suggestion, at first sight, sounds wrong-headed. There is a sense, no doubt, in which writing of any kind is a creative activity. But this is obviously not what is being suggested in linking the creative efforts of the philosopher with that of, say, the poet. Writing creatively, as I see it, is both to avoid the banal and the commonplace and to resist the pull of jargon, and those who do it well lift us out of a rut into which it is all too easy to fall. To write *well,* then, is to write creatively. The word 'creative' may have a certain mystique about it, but it is not, to my mind, a word we *need* to use in exploring the language of philosophy. The fact that our notions have rough edges and fringes, that we are not dealing with coins and counters but with living thoughts which naturally shade into each other, sets the stage for the work of articulation. Living ideas are poised in a delicate equilibrium. They are subject to unconscious pressures and to the influences of period, fashion and place – to none of which, however, thinking needs succumb. A great deal of human activity is carried out in resistance to pressures. Among these we have the inhibiting of ill-mannered behaviour in the interest of courtesy, the flouting of convention in the evolution of new mores, the heroic resistance to injustice,

---

[1] Hans-Georg Gadamer, *Wahrheit und Methode,* 2nd ed., p. 434.

to evil, of men of courage, Linguistic inventiveness (or creativity) is no less an indication of man's ability to swim against the stream. But, to develop the metaphor, such striving is *sustained* by the very buoyancy of the water, or, in our example, the habitus of speech. It is through one and the same language that we can resist the banal and the commonplace, and also the trappings that each discipline acquires for itself – jargon. The habitual is a crust we need to break through, whether it be the habitus of everyday speech or the acquired habitus of technical jargon. As far as breaking through the crust of the habitual is concerned, there is something very odd about the way linguistic analysts take familiarity of expression as a paradigm in the light of their exposure of subject/predicate ways of thinking, for these, after all, are highly familiar.

To say that philosophy and poetry intercede on behalf of language (especially in resisting jargon) is to speak in Heideggerian language. The poignancy of their task lies herein, that philosopher and poet have no alternative but to do this through language itself. The chief insight of importance which stems from twentieth-century interest in language is this: the dilemma for the metaphysician is not that reason issues in antinomies (for the temporary termini of thought are mostly multi-tracked) but that the language in which insight is expressed is the *same language* in which we talk about everyday things. We bog ourselves down and condemn ourselves to being 'grounded' in the everyday, not so much through an attachment to sense experience, to fact, as through an *underestimation* of experience, and, consequent on this, a failure to do justice to the infinitely subtle ways in which man can articulate that experience in language. This is why it was necessary to remind ourselves of what the poet does in a paradigmatic form. The poet is par excellence used to reading the signs, to perceiving the trans-empirical through the empirical.

Much of the corpus of linguistic analytical writing in recent years has been devoted to drawing distinctions between various modes of discourse. Useful as this was, especially in differentiating the formal from the non-formal disciplines, it served to obscure the ways in which there is a certain continuity between the articulations of *experience* which take a linguistic form. This continuity becomes especially manifest in the way metaphorical expressions derived from various fields can send philosophical thinking on its way. It is a continuity which is matched at the level of awareness by the shading of one experience into another, a phenomenon which belongs not only to the everyday but to those experiences commonly regarded as importantly distinct from it, that is, the aesthetic and the religious. We react to the sound of a hooter which recalls an air raid siren, the sight of gannets on Bass Rock, the cannon used in a war two generations ago, in a complex fashion, where initial perception branches out in multiple directions packed with a myriad intimations, each with its own horizon. This is the epistemic basis of those cosmological ways of thinking which those working in the classical rationalist tradition associated (and still associate) with analogical inference. But inference seems an inappropriate word for those outreaches of the human mind where one experience throws light on another, where we could indeed be groping were we relying on mere concepts, but where in fact our endeavours are fed from a wealth of sources, hinterland and context, and among them especially the resources that language has in abundance. There is, then, it seems to me, a profound link between the bonding of awareness which we experience in all ranges of experience, the bonding at the linguistic level of which our metaphoric transfers of meaning are the most clear evidence, and that bonding of Being which sustains them both. The experience of a gradual clarification of what one "wants to say", through the very saying of it, goes beyond the model-making of *dianoia*, the heuristic devices of picture-making. I here think of writing of high seriousness such as we associate with the labour of the philosopher and the poet and no doubt with that of certain other kinds of writer too.

Metaphysical language, like the language of poetry, possesses resonance, for in both cases the very manner of the saying is intrinsic to what is said. Such language is needed in all exploring where not steel nets, but antennae are what is called for. The language of philosophy is the language that sends philosophical thinking in its path. All along the route the quiet work of questioning, reallocating categories, feeling one's way, experiencing the shock of discovering the non-categorial, stretching uses of words, lassooing sportive ideas, pinpointing struggling images, goes on. Germinal insight and discourse nourish each other. And in any case the momentum of thought has nothing to do with moving belts on which we are propelled in a determined fashion. Now, if we are to throw light on the nature of metaphysical thinking it is necessary that the comparisons we make should have some pertinence. Since philosophy is a discipline where the manner of saying is intrinsic to what is said, we choose, at our peril, paradigms of statement whose lucidity stems from their triviality. It is for this reason that the condensed language of the poet repays study by the philosopher. The erecting of the light of common day into a paradigm happens to be the current fashion in empiricist circles. The irony is that it is not a paradigm which in the final analysis can get support from scientific thought. Much of scientific thinking concerns constructs which have scarcely a locus in the sensible world. We inhabit these new dimensions of the noösphere uneasily. Our enjoyment of science fiction (significantly the most popular literary genre in the West today) has the ring of laughter under extreme embarrassment about it; it calls to mind the act of the child who stands on his head in a large open space to console himself in one desperate gesture against the emptiness.

This brings us to the nature of reason, a matter with which our investigations began. A great deal of the history of philosophy is taken up with the definition of reason and the delimiting of its powers. From the vantage point of where we are now in the twentieth century any discussion of reason needs to take into account at least the following three considerations: that intelligence, knowing how as exhibited in action, and all our manipulative and practical skills, is as valid an expression of rationality as intellection: that the thinking involved in artistic creation is no less rational than the symbolic operations that belong to the formal disciplines of mathematics and logic; that all conscious operations have an unconscious hinterland. The misgivings that many people have about reason in our century are of a very different order from, say, the misgivings, and more, that Rousseau had. Let us see what misgivings arise today from the three considerations mentioned above. The association of rationality with manipulative skills, to a Bergson, ill suits it radically for entry into any other domain. Manipulation, and its attendant, calculation, does in a real sense often make redundant the use of linguistic skills. Wittgenstein's builder's analogy is a potent and unwitting illustration of this. The staccato announcement of a series of nouns suffices in order to get the job done. The *rationality* of the process at work in the composing of a fugue, the writing of an ode, should not have occasioned surprise to any one who reflects on the complex structure of each. But to liken philosophic activity, rational par excellence as this is reckoned to be, to artistic creation, as has been done many times in this study, believing as I do that philosophy belongs squarely in the humanities and is in no way a camp-follower of the natural sciences, is likely to raise strong feelings, to produce the impression that philosophy will thereby be sucked into the vortices of myth and mysticism. To find that all conscious processes, including the highly specialised operations of questioning, appraisal and criticism, trail inglorious clouds of unconscious activity has caused perhaps even more misgivings. Instead of coming to the conclusion that pure reason needs to have its wings clipped, we find that reason was never pure in the first place. The darkest shadows are now found to be cast not by opacities of speech (and certainly not by an excess of illumination) but by uncontrollable elements within man himself. Freudian teaching seems to chime in uncannily with the leading image of the *Phaedrus*, the image of the charioteer and the unruly horses, not at all the graceful tomb horses of the T'ang dynasty, or the gentle horses of Franz Marc's lyric canvases, but wild creatures bent on leading man to destruction. The thought of the consolations of salvation through sublimation hardly softens the sharp edge of this new version of the doctrine of original sin.

But does what Hume neatly described as the non-cogitative part of man's nature inherently subvert the pedigree of reason? Leibniz was almost alone in his own time in seeing how many structured the dimensions of consciousness were. Kant, the exponent of a very rational *Gesinnungsethik*, did not scorn to present in his first *Critique*, for expository purposes, a psychological 'layer' in order to lay bare a transcendental one. At a time when psychologism was not yet a bogey, Martineau could speak very suggestively and meaningfully of the springs of action. If we find it difficult to find in the unconscious mind, the childhood of man, a source of natural piety, if the Wordsworthian overtones have been irretrievably lost for twentieth-century man, we can yet find therein a matrix from which issues not only the dark and the terrible but material for the richest *metamorphoses* of which man is capable – the whole range of his symbolic activities through myth and language, to art, philosophy and religion. To say this is not to fall victim to reductionism. It is rather to be alive to the *difference* between the whence and the whither of thought. We can no longer regard reason as a faculty. We cannot even restrict it to an adaptive capacity which enables us to respond to an expanding world, for so many rational activities are not merely adaptive but genuinely innovative. The strange kinship that obtains between metaphysics and poetry gives us a clue, for both strive to articulate the bonding of Being of which each, in its own way, has an inkling, and in each case we have an activity which profoundly modifies the contours of man's self-knowledge. Both embody, in different ways, the *aspiration* of reason, an aspiration which enlists man's total psychic endowments. It is of this aspiration that the language of philosophy, no less than the language of poetry, *speaks*.

Index

Acquaintance, 5
Alice, Lewis Carroll, 5
Allemann, B., 110
Analogical inference, 134
Analytic philosophy, 43
Aquinas, Thomas, 102-3, 120
Argument, 62, 64, 71, 78, 80, 88, 93, 102, 113, 116, 126
    Philosophical discourse, 118-19
Aristotle, 4, 11, 12, 46, 47, 66, 120
    Philosophical treatise, 97-8
Aspiration
    Definition, 137
Austin, J.L., 77, 127
Ayer, A.J., 31, 64, 97

Bachelard, Gaston, 58
Bad metaphor, 49
Beardsley, Aubrey, 92, 94
Belief, 90
Bergson, Henri, 3, 4, 20, 24, 95, 97, 103, 135
Berkeley, George, 4, 42, 48, 66-7, 81, 93
Black, Max, 31, 50, 55, 119-20
Blanshard, Brand, 70
Bradley, Francis Herbert, 88
Bronson, 74
Brooks, Cleanth, 98
Browning, Elizabeth Barrett, 101
Burke, Kenneth, 56
Byron, George Gordon, 82

Cage, John, 35
Calder, 34
Camus, Albert, 101
Cezanne, Paul, 4
Coleridge, Samuel Taylor, 25, 99, 112
    Philosophy and poetry, 102-8
Collingwood, Robin George, 130
Concrete imagination, 47, 106
Conscious intention, 88, 92
Conscious mind, 80
Cornford, Francis Macdonald, 8

Cratylus, 9
Creative imagination, 25
Creativity, 55
Croce, Benedetto, 103
Cudworth, Ralph, 108

Dangerous metaphor, 74
Dante, 100
Darshana, 4
Darwin, Charles Robert, 6
Declared intention, 92
Descartes, Rene, 4, 66-7, 72
Descriptive metaphysics, 129
Dialectical reason, 11
Dilthey, Wilhelm, 3, 13, 27, 106
    Poetic and historical imagination, 21-6

Eliot, T.S., 97, 98
Enriched reason, 23
Etymology, 63-4, 109
Euripides, 97

Faber, Homo, 4
Fichte, Johann Gattlieb, 19, 20, 79
Figurative language, 3, 33, 72
Frege, Gottlob, 46, 131
    Metaphor, 57-8
Freud, Sigmund, 6, 14, 41, 46, 84, 91
    Desire, 80-1

Gadamer, 132
Geidegger, 118
Geographical metaphor, 98
Glaucon, 1, 40
Godwin, William, 106
Goethe, Johann W. Von, 14, 16
Gomperz, Theodore, 64
Gorgias, 10, 11
Gogh, Van, 114
Graphic language, 75
Greek poetry, 12
Guern, Michel Le, 58

INDEX

Gynt, Peer, 132

Hamann, Johann George, 14
Hardy, Alexander, 6
Hegel, George Wilhelm Friedrich, 17, 34, 48, 113
Heidegger, Martin, 78, 93, 99, 102-3
   Exploration of language, 107-16
   Linguistic imagination, 121-4
Heraclitus, 114
Herder, Johann Gottfried Von, 14, 15, 43
Herzberg, Alaxender, 79
Hesiod, 8, 10
Historical imagination, 6
Hobbes, Thomas, 66
Holderlin, Friedrich, 103
Holmesian, Sherlock, 45
Homer, 8, 10, 114
Huizinga, Johan, 29
Hume, David, 5, 20, 60, 80, 92, 135
Husserl, Edmund, 18, 22-3, 68, 87, 122, 131
   Figurative language, 72-4

Imagination, 74, 85, 89, 99, 103-7, 127
   Meaning, 5-7
   And Metaphors, 57-8
   And reason, 9-26
   Or reason, 15-16
Induction, 42
Inference, 134
Intention, 92-4

James, William, 53, 79
Jaspers, Karl, 124
Jung, Carl, 8
Junger, Ernst, 110

Kandinsky, Vasili, 34
Kant, Immanual, 9, 34, 54, 80, 87, 93, 104, 106, 108, 135-6
   Imagination, 15-22
   Metaphor and meaning, 46-7
   Metaphorical discourse, 57-60
   Metaphysical thinking, 68-72
   Metaphysics, 13-14
   Philosophic and poetic discourse, 119-20
   Philosophic thought, 42-3
   Philosophy and arts, 4-7
Kierkegaard, Saren Aabye, 103, 113, 120
Kroner, Richard, 7

Langer, Susanne, 103

Language
   Definition, 9
Language games, 3, 29-34, 45, 83-4, 109
   Metaphor, 32, 84
Language strata, 45
Lazerowitz, Morris, 3, 4, 45, 81, 87-94
Leibniz, G.W., 14, 48, 135-6
Lessing, Gotthod Ephrain, 104
Linear discourse, 119
Linguistic imagination, 26, 35, 44, 45, 47, 62, 117, 122-3
Literature and philosophy, 97
Living metaphor, 58
Locke, John, 46, 63, 68
Lonergan, 22, 118
Lowith, Karl, 110

Mace, C.A., 97
Maritain, Jacques, 99, 103
Martineau, Harriet, 135-6
Marx, Karl, 5, 6, 21
Metaphorical discourse, 52, 54-61, 70
Metaphors, 3, 8, 9, 11, 16, 28, 34, 37-9. 41, 73, 77, 79, 84-9, 92-5, 102, 105, 109, 111, 117, 120, 125, 133
   And meaning, 45-61
   And philosophical discourse, 62-9
Metaphysical discourse, 97, 99
Metaphysical language, 134
Metaphysics, 6, 13, 47, 63, 97, 112, 115
   And poetry, 137
Milton, John, 100
Mimesis, 10, 11
Mind, 78, 89, 106
Moore, Addison Webster, 127-8
Mundle, 31
Munz, Peter, 8
Murdoch, Iris, 97
Myths, 9, 46, 78, 112, 130-1
   And language, 137

Newton, Isaac, 16, 66-7
Nietzsche, Friedrich Wilhelm, 6, 100
Novel metaphor, 49
Nowottny, Winifred, 52

Oakeshott, 55
Obscurity, 39
Ogden, George Washington, 6
Olympus, Mt., 10
Opacity, 36
Open texture, 40-2

INDEX

Ordinary language, 1
Original intention, 92

Parmenides, 114
Pepper, S.C., 65
Perception, 42
Phaedo, 10
Phaedrus, 10
Philosopher
  Definition, 1-2, 40
Philosophical arguments, 37, 118-19
Philosophical discourse, 62, 95, 102, 117-20, 125
Philosophical language, 2-3, 7, 101
Philosophical metaphor, 3, 102, 119
Philosophical prose, 3
Philosophical theories, 85-9, 91
Philosophy
  Definition, 8
  And literature, 80, 98
  And poetry, 3, 4, 7, 12, 20, 98-100, 107, 114-16, 133
  And religion, 2
  And science, 1, 2, 4
Pindar, 99, 108, 114
Pintus, Kurt, 108
Plato, 1, 4, 8, 9, 10, 11, 12, 92, 97, 101, 114
Poetic discourse, 111, 119
Poetic imagination, 100, 106
Poetic language, 2-3
Poetic metaphor, 57
Poetry and philosophy, 2, 17, 20, 101, 106
Porosity, 40
Price, H.H., 81
Prichard, Katherine Susannah, 93
Productive reason, 18
Pure reason, 9, 18, 54, 104

Reason, 6, 9, 11-26, 58, 92, 105-7, 117, 132-7
  And imagination, 6-7, 100
  With imagination, 62
Revisionary metaphysics, 129
Richards, I.A., 6, 49, 63
Rickert, Heinrich, 21
Ricoeur, Paul, 48, 57-8, 95, 98
Rilke, Rainer Maria, 114
Robbe-Grillet, 101
Robinson, James Harvey, 79-80
Root, Bass, 133
Root metaphor, 65

Rousseau, J.J., 14, 15, 20, 99, 135
Russell, Bertrand, 4, 28, 91
Ryle Gilbert, 68, 75, 77-8, 85, 93, 101, 128

Sapir-Whorf, 82, 130
Sartre, Jean-Paul, 101
Schelling, Friedrich Wilhelm Joseph Von, 20
Scientific imagination, 6
Scientific language, 56
Schleiermacher, Friedrich Ernst Daniel, 25
Schoenberg, Arnold, 33-4
Schopenhauer, Arthur, 20, 103
Shakespeare, William, 104
Socrates, 1, 9, 11. 14
Sophocles, Evangelinus Apostolides, 97, 114
Speculative impulse, 6
Speculative metaphysics, 129
Spinoza, Baruch, 66
Stein, Gertrude, 35
Strawson, Peter Feredich, 5, 16, 93, 129
Subsequent intension, 92
Subversion, 79, 95

Technical language, 1
Tetens, 25, 95
Thread metaphor, 32
Topographical metaphor, 76
Tool-kit metaphor, 31-2, 45
Tools metaphor, 32
Trakl, 114
Truth, 43, 104, 113, 115, 121-2, 126
  Definition, 39
Turbayne, C.M., 65-6, 68, 75, 81

Unconscious intension, 88, 92
Unconscious mind, 80, 88, 135
Undeclared intention, 92
Urmson, 128

Valery, Paul Ambroise, 29, 43, 101
Voltaire, 99

Waismann, Friedrich, 1, 3, 31, 37-44, 53, 55, 122
Warnock, 128
Weil, Simone, 102
Whitehead, Alfred North, 103
Wilhelm, Kaiser, 82
Wimsatt, 92, 94
Wisdom, J.O., 67, 77, 81, 85
Wisdom, John, 81, 91
Wittgenstein, Ludwig Josef Johann, 14, 38,

Wittgenstein (*Contd.*)
  42, 64, 74, 110, 128
  Language games and linguistic imagination, 27-34
  Philosophical ideas, 81-90

Wolff, Christian Von, 14, 20
Wordsworth, William, 101, 105-7
Wrong anologies, 36-7

Young, Edward, 99